Praise for *Comfort the Grieving*

Few have attempted to offer comfort to those who grieve, and fewer have been as successful as Pastor Paul Tautges in this much-needed book. This wonderful little volume is a veritable anthology of practical helps for those who are grieving and for those who minister to their needs. I recommend it as a book for all deacons, elders, pastors, and laypersons. This important tool should be thoughtfully read if we are to minister wisely and effectively to those in our fellowship who will eventually face such times.

*Dr. Walter C. Kaiser Jr., president emeritus
of Gordon-Conwell Theological Seminary*

Paul Tautges gives pastors and other compassionate caregivers a unique book that is thoroughly biblical and immensely practical. He teaches us how to biblically comfort hurting and dying people, offering pertinent Scriptures, hymns, and poems to use, as well as providing a plan for ministering to those left behind following the death of a loved one. We find here solid ideas for preparing funeral messages that not only comfort the grieving but also challenge the lost with a clear gospel message. I know of no book like *Comfort the Grieving*. Many how-to books are shallow and devoid of deep theological content. This excellent book is an exception.

*Curtis C. Thomas, pastor for over fifty years
and author of* Life in the Body of Christ

Paul Tautges is a man with a mission to minister to the brokenhearted. He carefully offers a blend of sensitive concern with a proclamation of the gospel in clear, honest language. His thoughts on the theology of grief, as well as the sermons and practical charts in this book, will surely be helpful to those pastors who search for ways to improve this aspect of their own ministries. This book gives us a glimpse into the heart of a pastor who possesses a love for his flock, a sound grasp of the Scriptures, and a calling to comfort the hurting in a biblical, compassionate way.

Deborah Howard, RN, certified hospice and palliative nurse and author of Sunsets: Reflections for Life's Final Journey *and* Where Is God in All of This?

Within the pages of *Comfort the Grieving* we find biblical, insightful, and practical advice for serving those who grieve. Written with the tenderness and understanding of a gentle pastor, this book is a helpful manual for those who guide others through the valley of the shadow of death. I hope it gains wide distribution!

Dr. Les Lofquist, executive director of IFCA International

COMFORT THE GRIEVING

REVISED AND UPDATED

**Ministering God's Grace
in Times of Loss**

PAUL TAUTGES

ZONDERVAN

Comfort the Grieving
Copyright © 2014 by Paul Tautges

Previously published in 2009 by Day One Publications under the title
Comfort Those Who Grieve

This title is also available as a Zondervan ebook.
Visit www.zondervan.com/ebooks.

Requests for information should be addressed to:
Zondervan, 3900 *Sparks Dr. SE, Grand Rapids, Michigan 49546*

Library of Congress Cataloging-in-Publication Data

Tautges, Paul.
    Comfort the grieving : ministering God's grace in times of loss / Paul
    Tautges ; Brian Croft, series editor.
        pages cm
    Includes bibliographical references.
    ISBN 978-0-310-51933-1 (softcover)
    1. Church work with the bereaved. 2. Pastoral theology. I. Title.
BV4330.T38 2015
259'.6--dc23   2014023086

Cover design and illustration: Jay Smith—Juicebox Designs
Interior design: Matthew Van Zomeren

Printed in the United States of America

HB 01.30.2024

To the memory of Jean Pitz,
a dear sister in the Lord,
who always had a word of encouragement for this
preacher of the gospel
and who would never exchange her place in glory for
anything this world has to offer

&

to hospice caregivers everywhere,
who sacrificially give of themselves from the heart
in order to help others comfortably live through the
experience of death

CONTENTS

PART 2: PREACHING THAT COMFORTS

FOREWORD

SOME OF THE MOST VALUABLE LESSONS I ever learned as a pastor, lessons that are affirmed year after year, happen in hospital rooms and funeral homes. I have watched sweet elderly saints take their last breath while I'm holding their hand and praying for them. I have won over enemies after visiting them as they recover in a hospital room. I have seen despair turn to hope while talking about Christ as I've sat with a grieving widow at a funeral visitation. These pivotal moments for fruitful ministry exist because the hospital room and the funeral home accomplish something few life moments can. They remind us of our frailty and brokenness. They jolt our hearts into reality when we are tempted to believe we are invincible. They press us to focus on eternal things when we want to live in the temporal.

And yet, ironically, these are places many pastors try to avoid today. Why? Well, this kind of ministry is hard work. It is not glamorous. It requires us to engage our hearts in a way that makes many of us uncomfortable. It involves assuming burdens that are painful to bear. Sometimes no one knows you are doing this ministry—except for God and the people you visit. But these types of visits are at the core of our calling as pastors who shepherd God's flock until the Chief Shepherd returns (1 Peter 5:4). And I'm convinced that one of the best ways to recover these essential aspects of pastoral ministry is to equip pastors so they can better care for those who are grieving.

Comfort the Grieving

That is why I am excited about this book. I'm excited because the content and structure are well suited for equipping pastors and others to comfort those who grieve. After discussing the biblical foundations that show us where our hope comes from in times of grief, Paul Tautges goes on to describe various ways in which a pastor can minister this hope to others. The second section includes sample sermons, and the appendixes offer practical helps. There is advice on writing notes and using songs, and the book contains charts to help in scheduling visits and contacts in the first year of bereavement. *Comfort the Grieving* contains a concise, clear introduction to the theology and tools you need to shepherd grieving people well.

The second reason I am excited about this book is that it is a key resource in the Practical Shepherding series. One book in the series, *Visit the Sick*, addresses how to extend care to people through the struggles of sickness, pain, and affliction. Another book, *Conduct Gospel-Centered Funerals*, addresses the immediate circumstances surrounding a death, including the preparation of a funeral sermon and logistics of working with funeral homes. Although hospitals and funeral homes are key places to do ministry, they are not the only places where grief is experienced. Much of the grieving process requires extended care that takes place long after the immediate circumstances of the hospital and funeral home.

Comfort the Grieving is a wonderful complement to these two books. It fills in the gaps while affirming the wisdom and practical helps they offered. In addition, I highly recommend the author to you. Paul Tautges is a faithful man of God and a shepherd of God's people who has tenderly comforted many with the hope of the gospel and writes with a seasoned wisdom needed to instruct others. My prayer is that you will be blessed by his wisdom and faithfulness to the Scriptures.

Brian Croft, January 2014

INTRODUCTION

Why should I feel discouraged, why should
    the shadows come,
Why should my heart be lonely, and long
    for heav'n and home,
When Jesus is my portion? My constant
    Friend is He:
His eye is on the sparrow, and I know He
    watches me.

Civilla D. Martin, 1905

AFTER TWO DECADES of pastoral ministry in the same church and several years of service as a hospital chaplain, I've been exposed to grief and death, far more so than the average pastor. During those years, I wondered if someday I might write about my experiences, but I confess I was unprepared when the opportunity finally arrived.

What you are reading is not just a typical book. The writing has been an important part of my own grieving process. In his helpful booklet *Grief: Finding Hope Again*, Paul Tripp writes, "Death is an emotionally volatile event that is painful in unexpected ways. Death digs up buried memories. It brings some people together and drives others apart. It begins some things and ends others. Death mixes happiness with sadness."[1] In my own experience, I've learned that death provides an opportunity for us not only to minister to others but also to experience personal growth as ministers. As we offer comfort to others, we must also learn to grieve.

Even as I sat down to work on the final version of this book, my friend's father died. Within a couple of hours, he was in the presence of Jesus. Learning to walk through the painful valley of the shadow of death along with our church members is a vital part of a shepherd's calling. Death is painfully real. We would have to be cold, calloused, or uninvolved in people's lives not to be affected by it. With compassion, we must learn how to offer Christ-centered comfort to those who grieve. This priority has been freshly implanted in my mind as I've worked on this book, as God has brought several members of my congregation face-to-face with death.

The gospel portion of the book of Isaiah begins with these words: "Comfort, comfort my people, says your God" (Isaiah 40:1). Isaiah has earned the nickname "the evangelical prophet" because of his emphasis on the good news of the coming Messiah — the hope and strong comfort of Israel. With reference to this verse, Warren Wiersbe explains, "The English word 'comfort' comes from two Latin words that together mean 'with strength.' When Isaiah says to us, 'Be comforted!' it is not a word of pity but of power. God's comfort does not weaken us; it strengthens us. God is not indulging us but empowering us."[2]

Overwhelmed by their failure and by the sin which brought about severe chastisement, the people of God were in desperate need of hope — the hope of God's pardon. Verse 2 continues: "Speak tenderly to Jerusalem, and proclaim to her that her hard service has been completed, that her sin has been paid for, that she has received from the Lord's hand double for all her sins."

The hope that Isaiah gives is rooted in God's relationship to Israel as his people: "Comfort *my* people, says *your* God." Though his people's sin was indeed worthy of a double portion of divine discipline, God was not about to turn his back on them. He would fulfill the covenant that he had made with them. Later, through the mouth of Jeremiah, God again dispenses hope in the midst of Israel's pain: " 'For I know the plans that I have for you,' declares the Lord, 'plans to prosper you and not to harm you, plans to give you hope and a future' " (Jeremiah 29:11). Both prophets provided Messiah-centered comfort by turning their focus away from their past and present, and toward the future hope of the promised kingdom.

Since we live *after* the cross of Calvary, we can refer to this as "Christ-centered comfort," but the nature of the comfort God offers to us today is much the same. The strength of God's comfort does not come from his ability to change our present circumstances (which he can do if he chooses). Rather, God's comfort comes from his promise to us in Christ that the glory we will one day share with him far outweighs our present suffering (Romans 8:18; Philippians 1:6; 2 Corinthians 4:17).

Christ-centered comfort is the only true comfort. Any comfort we give to people that lies outside the hope of the gospel is temporary at best and deceptive at worst. If we merely dispense earthly comfort to those who are suffering and fail to point them to the only true source of comfort, Jesus Christ, we can easily deceive them into thinking that God is on their side when, in fact, he may not be. If they are unbelievers, then they are still God's enemies, and we have offered them no lasting comfort at all until we point them to the "man of sorrows" who is "acquainted with grief" (Isaiah 53:3 NASB).

The gospel offers us Christ-centered hope that enables us to face the reality of death head-on. It holds forth the gift of eternal life that Jesus purchased with his own blood. If we fail to gently speak the truth of the gospel in times of grief, we have not made death a servant to God's purposes. In our words of encouragement, we must seize each divinely ordained ministry opportunity to utilize earthly pain by redirecting people to focus on eternal matters. Joni Eareckson Tada and Steve Estes write in their book *When God Weeps*, "Earth's pain keeps crushing our hopes, reminding us this world can never satisfy; only heaven can. And every time we begin to nestle too comfortably on this planet, God cracks open the locks of the dam to allow an ice-cold splash of suffering to wake us from our spiritual slumber."[3] We must not waste these precious—and painful—occasions that are given to us for the demonstration of mercy and the advantage of the gospel.

PART 1

A MINISTRY OF COMFORT

CHAPTER 1

GOD IS OUR REFUGE

The Biblical Foundation for Our Comfort

WEATHER SATELLITES ORBIT THE EARTH, tracking weather systems as they move across the globe. These satellites provide advance warning of changing weather conditions and alert us to possible dangers. Television channels and smart phone apps convey this information and allow us to track the weather. And knowing the future in this way provides us with a bit of comfort, doesn't it? It helps us to plan ahead so we can avoid discomfort and danger.

Often, we wish God would provide a similar advance warning in the storms of life — the difficulties he sends our way. God typically does not warn us ahead of time. Though he does not hide the truth that we will face troubles and hardships in this life, in a general sense (John 16:33; 1 Peter 4:12), he does not reveal the particular details of our individual suffering. If he did, we would likely be inclined to walk by sight rather than by faith. We would try to control our own lives, avoiding the pain rather than learning to trust him and his goodness and his promises. Above all, we must learn that he is in control. And when the fierce storms of life come, we must not be ashamed to run to God and find refuge in him.

God's people need an anchor to hold on to during the storms of life. Ministers of God's grace must learn how to help people find that anchor by establishing a solid doctrinal foundation for their people. They need to allow gospel truth to grow deep roots through regular preaching that helps people trust in God's sovereignty over every event of life, along with a solid grasp of his personal care for each of his children — from the day of their birth to the day of their death. Deborah Howard, a hospice caregiver, writes about the importance of knowing and believing that God is good and in control: "We must have the essential faith and trust in God *before* our hearts are broken. Then we will possess the tools needed to understand and deal with the situation *without being devastated*." [4] Faithful ministers must begin by preparing God's people to face life's dangers and help them develop a vigorous faith in the sovereign God of comfort.

To minister God's grace in times of loss, we must be truth-filled witnesses and loving shepherds. We must faithfully speak the word of God so that our fellow Christians have a rock-solid foundation on which to build their lives. Yet we must also be sensitive shepherds who walk our sheep through the dark valley of suffering — even death itself — as they hold to the comfort of God. As we serve them with compassion, God will use us to instill a biblical hope and confidence that matches the psalmist's:

God Is Our Refuge

Even though I walk
    through the darkest valley,
I will fear no evil,
    for you are with me;
your rod and your staff,
    they comfort me.

Psalm 23:4

Preaching cannot be separated from pastoral care. On the contrary, it is a vital part of our care. We provide pastoral care through sensitive preaching, and nothing accomplishes this more effectively than regular preaching on this twofold reality: God's absolute sovereignty *and* his tender care for his own. We find this balance throughout the psalms, inspired words that were birthed out of human pain and tragedy.

The writer of an old hymn declares, "How firm a foundation, ye saints of the Lord, is laid for your faith in his excellent Word!"[5] These words complement those of the apostle Peter, who assures us that "we also have the prophetic message as something completely reliable" — something even more significant than the most dramatic spiritual experience (2 Peter 1:19). There is no time in our lives, as believers, when this secure base of biblical truth is more necessary than when we stand at the door of death.

God, the Foundation of Comfort

Psalm 46 offers a foundation for this ministry of comfort, along with some helpful application. The primary emphasis of Psalm 46 is not on trying to guess when and where the storms will come. Instead, the emphasis is on knowing the God who is the source of protection and rest in the midst of the storms. God rarely indicates when a storm is coming. But he does provide protection and comfort in the storm. We must learn to "hide" ourselves in God (Psalm 143:9), finding our strength, our peace, and our rest *in God* and his promises, even as our souls wrestle with pain and hurt inside. God alone is the One who can meet our deepest needs, and he promises to nurture us and teach us what it really means to trust him through every trial of life. The psalmist writes these words:

> God is our refuge and strength,
> > an ever-present help in trouble.
> Therefore we will not fear, though the earth give way
> > and the mountains fall into the heart of the sea,
> though its waters roar and foam
> > and the mountains quake with their surging.
> There is a river whose streams make glad the city of God,
> > the holy place where the Most High dwells.
> God is within her, she will not fall;
> > God will help her at break of day.
> Nations are in uproar, kingdoms fall;
> > he lifts his voice, the earth melts.
> The Lord Almighty is with us;
> > the God of Jacob is our fortress.
> Come and see what the Lord has done,
> > the desolations he has brought on the earth.
> He makes wars cease
> > to the ends of the earth.
> He breaks the bow and shatters the spear;
> > he burns the shields with fire.
> He says, "Be still, and know that I am God;
> > I will be exalted among the nations,

I will be exalted in the earth."
The LORD Almighty is with us;
   the God of Jacob is our fortress.

                                        Psalm 46

As we take a closer look at what the psalmist says here, we see that God is our "refuge." God is a place of shelter for us, a place of safety. Psalm 46 isn't the first place this imagery appears in the Bible. Scripture provides several images of the surety of God's loving care for us in times of fear and sorrow. For example, Moses paints a picture of God's strong and loving care when he writes, "The eternal God is your refuge, and underneath are the everlasting arms" (Deuteronomy 33:27). The phrase "everlasting arms" illustrates the Creator's strong protection and tender care. Another image that helps us appreciate God's care for his children is the reference to God's "wings" in Psalm 57 as David is fleeing from Saul. At that time, David prays:

Have mercy on me, my God, have mercy on me,
   for in you I take refuge.
I will take refuge in the shadow of your wings
   until the disaster has passed.

                                        Psalm 57:1

Moses also makes use of this image in Psalm 91:4:

He will cover you with his feathers,
   and under his wings you will find refuge;
   his faithfulness will be your shield and rampart.

Both Moses and David see God's care and protection as similar to that of a protective mother bird. In times of trouble, God spreads out his wings of love to guard his children so that "no harm will overtake you" (Psalm 91:10). Jesus himself drew on this image when he said, "Jerusalem, Jerusalem, you who kill the prophets and stone those sent to you, how often I have longed to gather your children together, as a hen gathers her chicks under her wings, and you were not willing" (Matthew 23:37).

God is our refuge, offering us his tender care and protection, and God is also our "strength." He puts his power into action for us. Knowing this, we should "look to the LORD and his strength; seek his face always" (1 Chronicles 16:11). His strength works *for us* in our times of weakness. In fact, according to the apostle Paul, the strength of God is somehow perfected when we are weak and dependent on God (2 Corinthians 12:9). It is when we feel as if the rug has been pulled out from underneath us that we begin to recognize just how weak we truly are. In these times, the strength of God is made perfect and complete in our lives. We experience the fullness of God's strength only as we are humbled in our weakness.

The psalmist also reminds us that God is our "ever-present help" in times of sorrow and fear. God doesn't respond to us from a distance. Rather, he draws near to us. His omnipresence is personal and active. He moves into action on our behalf. He is near to those who run to him, who turn to him as their refuge and strength. This leads the author of Psalm 46 to assure us of two results that come from hiding in God.

1. Because God is our refuge, we are freed from fear (verses 2–7). When God is big, our circumstances are small. We no longer need to fear our present circumstances or worry about the future. Because God is our refuge, "we will not fear." Proverbs 14:26 adds this: "Whoever fears the LORD has a secure fortress, and for their children it will be a refuge." If you have experienced the pain of grief and suffering, you know you don't have the strength to face your fears alone. But you aren't alone. God gives us strength when we draw near to him. When the Lord is our refuge, we will have strength to face our fears, even the fear of our own death or the death of a loved one. Jesus exhorts us in Matthew 10:28, "Do not be afraid of those who kill the body but cannot kill the soul. Rather, be afraid of the One who can destroy both soul and body in hell." When a close loved one returns from a visit to the cancer specialist and tells us that nothing more can be done, that "it's only a matter of time," our hearts will immediately cry out in fear and grief. The pain is real, but we need not give in to fear and despair. God is our refuge, especially in these times, and "therefore we will not fear." *Trusting God dispels all other fears because only he is sovereign over death.* We know that death is not final, that God is in control, and that he has promised us ultimate victory in Jesus. As we grow in our love for God and his love for us, this "perfect love drives out fear" (1 John 4:18).

What is fear? A simple definition is that fear is misplaced trust. Instead of trusting God, we trust something else, often ourselves. We trust our own ability to control our future and our immediate circumstances. Faith requires a positive loss of control, a relinquishing of our supposed authority over our lives, and a willing surrender of our control to God, who possesses ultimate control, along with infinite goodness and wisdom. Dustin Shramek gives a vivid illustration of the faith that clings to God, especially when we don't have the strength to hang on:

Experiencing grief and pain is like falling off a cliff. Everything has been turned upside down, and we are no longer in control. As we fall, we see one *and only one* tree that is growing out from the rock face. So we grab hold of it and cling to it with all our might. This tree is our holy God. He alone can keep us from falling headfirst to our doom. There simply aren't any other trees to grab. So we cling to this tree (the holy God) with all our might.

But what we didn't realize is that when we fell and grabbed the tree our arm actually became entangled in the branches, so that in reality, the tree is holding us. We hold on to keep from falling, but what we don't realize is that we can't fall because the tree has us. We are safe. God, in his holiness, is keeping us and showing mercy to us. We may not be aware of it, but it is true. He is with us even in the deepest and darkest pit.[6]

When circumstances are beyond our control, and seem to be working against us, we must hold on to the truth that God loves us and that there is nothing that can separate us from that love if we are in Christ: "I am convinced that neither death nor life, neither angels nor demons, neither the present nor the future, nor any powers, neither height nor depth, nor anything else in all creation, will be able to separate us from the love of God that is in Christ Jesus our Lord" (Romans 8:38 – 39). This declaration by the apostle Paul is not a generic assurance that God will help people in pain, as it is sometimes used; it is a promise made to those who place their faith and trust in Jesus Christ.

When I struggle with fears, I often drive a few miles to the shore of Lake Michigan, one of the Great Lakes, and spend time listening to the waves and reflecting on the awesome power of God. When a storm comes in, the waves will rage and threaten to damage the docked sailboats and yachts; yet the water in the harbor remains relatively calm because of the breakwater. The boats that rest in the harbor are secure because the rock wall is designed to hold back the threatening waves.

Living in the harbor doesn't shield us from experiences of grief and pain, but it does mean we can have peace in the midst of the storms because we have access to God's protecting power. We are no longer at the mercy of circumstances; we cling to the mercy of God. Using the imagery of waves, James Bruce writes about the very real pain of grief and the hope that comes when we have a strong anchor:

> Real grief is not easily comforted. It comes like ocean waves rushing up the sand, subsiding back, only to roll in again. These waves vary in size, frequency, and intensity. Some are small, lapping up around the feet. Others are stronger; they foam the water around you and cause you to stagger. Then there are the overwhelming waves with an undertow that can turn your world upside down and drag you out into deep waters. In times such as those, the mourner desperately needs an anchor.[7]

That anchor we hold to is God. As we trust in him, we remain unshakable, safe, and secure in his tender care. No matter how difficult our storms may be, we can endure them with inner calm and joy. The author of Psalm 46 writes, "There is a river whose streams make glad the city of God, the holy place where the Most High dwells" (verse 4). Again, we are assured of the Lord's presence with us everywhere: "God is within her, she will not fall; God will help her at break of day" (verse 5). It is peaceful in the city of God, where he dwells. And if we dwell with God, we know that even when circumstances are beyond our control, we are exactly where God wants us to be. In our grief, we learn to trust him, the One who delights in coming to our aid.

2. Because God is our refuge, we are freed from anxiety (verses 8 – 11). In light of this assurance of God's protection, the psalmist tells us in verse 10 that we must "be still, or "cease striving," as the NASB translates it. This is the second lesson of the psalm. The Hebrew word translated "be still" or "cease striving" means to sink or relax, to let go or abandon. "Striving" is a term that typically refers to warfare, so the admonition can be stated this way: "Be at peace."

According to Philippians 4:6 – 7, the means of gaining this God-given, protective peace is *prayer*: "Do not be anxious about anything [do not fret], but in every situation, by prayer and petition, with thanksgiving, present your requests to God. And the peace of God, which transcends all understanding, will guard your hearts and your minds in Christ Jesus." When we bring our fears and worries to God in prayer, he sends us his peace to stand like a sentry at the door of our heart and our mind. God's peace is a secure deadbolt against anxiety.

God's peace comes as we remember the powerful deeds of God. These provide us with an essential weapon in the battle against fear. Verses 8 to 10 instruct us:

> Come and see what the LORD has done,
> the desolations he has brought on the earth.
> He makes wars cease
> to the ends of the earth.

He breaks the bow and shatters the spear;
  he burns the shields with fire.
He says, "Be still, and know that I am God."

In other words, "Stop worrying! I am God; you are not! I will get the victory. Stop acting as if you are in charge. Stop, relax, and rest in me. I am your God. I will be your peace." This spiritual rest is not something we passively experience; it is a demonstration of an active faith. Writing about our "rest" in God and his word to us, Walter Kaiser teaches, "The word for 'rest' (*manoah*) is related in Hebrew to the word for 'comfort' (*menahem*) and is a word possessing considerable theological weight. The 'rest' of God is *a state of being that we enter into by belief*."[8] In other words, unlike physical sleep, spiritual rest in God actually involves an active choice. We must end our worrying and instead replace those worries with confidence that God is God and is therefore in full control. As fears threaten to overtake us and destroy our peace, we must *actively* rest in God by faith.

We rest by remembering his mighty deeds: "Come and see what the LORD has done." When we are tempted to worry, we must remember the great works that God has done—not only in the earth, but in our own lives. Rest involves reflecting on the many ways in which God has providentially cared for us, satisfied our needs, and demonstrated his power, love, and grace. This is a direct antidote to our worries and is the same principle Jesus taught his disciples in Matthew 6:25–34:

> "Therefore [because you cannot serve two masters] I tell you, do not worry about your life, what you will eat or

drink; or about your body, what you will wear. Is not life more than food, and the body more than clothes? Look at the birds of the air [see the works of God!]; they do not sow or reap or store away in barns, and yet your heavenly Father feeds them. Are you not much more valuable than they? Can any one of you by worrying add a single hour to your life?

"And why do you worry about clothes? See how the flowers of the field grow [see the works of God!]. They do not labor or spin. Yet I tell you that not even Solomon in all his splendor was dressed like one of these. If that is how God clothes the grass of the field [see the works of God!], which is here today and tomorrow is thrown into the fire, will he not much more clothe you—you of little faith? So do not worry, saying, 'What shall we eat?' or 'What shall we drink?' or 'What shall we wear?' For the pagans run after all these things, and your heavenly Father knows that you need them. But seek first his kingdom and his righteousness, and all these things will be given to you as well. Therefore do not worry about tomorrow, for tomorrow will worry about itself. Each day has enough trouble of its own."

Worry will hinder our faith, cloud our focus, and rob us of our ability to see clearly the good works of the Lord. Worrying brings us no benefit. Someone has well said, "Worry is like a rocking chair. It will give you something to do, but it won't get you anywhere."[9] And worst of all, worry is an enemy of faith. Instead of fretting over that which we cannot control, we need to learn to quietly rest in the One who is sovereign over every atom in the universe. Jesus Christ, the omnipotent Creator, "is before all things, and in him all things hold together" (Colossians 1:17).

God Is Our Refuge

Psalm 46 ends by repeating a key truth for us: "The LORD Almighty is with us; the God of Jacob is our fortress." This truth was already stated in verse 7—and in verse 1 in different words: "God is . . . an ever-present help in trouble." By stating the same truth three times in slightly different ways, the psalmist is making a point: *We must never forget, when we are in the midst of our storms, that God's presence is real.* He is not far away. He is very near to us in our grief and suffering.

Do you believe this? God says he will never leave you or forsake you. No matter how painful your trial may become, God will always remain with you if you belong to him in Christ. This truth is beautifully communicated in a poem based on Isaiah 43:2 titled "When Thou Passest Through the Waters." May it encourage you as it has me.

> Is there any heart discouraged as it journeys on its way?
> Does there seem to be more darkness than there is
>   of sunny day?
> Oh, it's hard to learn the lesson, as we pass beneath the rod,
> That the sunshine and the shadow serve alike the will of God;
> But there comes a word of promise like the promise
>   in the bow—
> That however deep the waters, they shall never overflow.
>
> When the flesh is worn and weary, and the spirit is depressed,
> And temptations sweep upon it, like a storm
>   on ocean's breast,
> There's a haven ever open for the tempest-driven bird;
> There's a shelter for the tempted in the promise of the Word;
> For the standard of the Spirit shall be raised against the foe,

Comfort the Grieving

And however deep the waters, they shall never overflow.

When a sorrow comes upon you that no other soul can share,
And the burden seems too heavy for the human heart to bear,
There is One whose grace can comfort if you'll give Him
an abode;
There's a Burden-Bearer ready if you'll trust Him
with your load;
For the precious promise reaches to the depth of human woe,
That however deep the waters, they shall never overflow.

When the sands of life are ebbing and I know that death
is near;
When I'm passing through the valley, and the way seems
dark and drear;
I will reach my hand to Jesus, in His bosom I shall hide,
And 'twill only be a moment till I reach the other side;
It is then the fullest meaning of the promise I shall know.
"When thou passest through the waters, they shall
never overflow."[10]

CHAPTER 2

THE DEATH OF A BELIEVER

Ministering with Pastoral Tenderness

It is not death to die,
To leave this weary road,
And 'midst the brotherhood on high
To be at home with God ...
Jesus, Thou Prince of Life!
Thy chosen cannot die;
Like Thee, they conquer in the strife,
To reign with Thee on high.

H. A. César Malan,
"It Is Not Death to Die"

THE DEATH OF A CHURCH MEMBER is a difficult experience for any church. Scripture teaches that "there are many parts, but one body" (1 Corinthians 12:20). Like each part of the human body, each member of the church needs all the other parts for the church's proper health and function: "The eye cannot say to the hand, 'I don't need you!' And the head cannot say to the feet, 'I don't need you!'" (verse 21). The reality of this interdependence is felt when fellow church members are in the midst of suffering. Grief within a church is not a sign of weakness; rather, it is an indicator that the church is functioning as God designed it to function. For "if one part suffers, every part suffers with it" (verse 26). A pastor must be sensitive to the needs of the flock that God has called him to shepherd. He must be ready at a moment's notice to shift gears in his preaching to address the pain of his sheep.

Jean Pitz was a member of our church family, a vital part of our body. In July 2007, she was diagnosed with cancer, and God's people began praying. We called on the Lord and pleaded with him to spare her life. Our limited knowledge pointed to Jean's imminent death. But we also knew that with God, all things are possible. So we held all-night prayer vigils for our dear sister. And God answered our prayers. He raised up Jean to the bewilderment of the medical establishment and gave her back to us for nine more months. Her family enjoyed one more Thanksgiving, one more Christmas, and one more Easter together. God blessed us with the honor of serving her and walking through the dark valley of cancer with her. And Jean walked the way with joy and faith. She had a peace that could only be explained by the salvation that Jesus had purchased for her. Nine months later, she beat the rest of us to the finish line, and on April 12, 2008, her fight with cancer came to an end. We are confident she is now casting her crowns at her Savior's feet alongside believers of previous ages as she worships. God brought Jean home to share his eternal peace, rest, and joy. Our church grieved and our grieving was good and right.

The Death of a Believer

Christians need not hide their grief. In fact, they should embrace it. The Bible is filled with examples of people who grieved at the death of a loved one. Abraham grieved the death of Sarah, his wife. In Genesis 23:2 we read, Sarah "died at Kiriath Arba (that is, Hebron) in the land of Canaan, and Abraham went to mourn for Sarah and to weep over her." The New Testament also reveals that godly men grieved the death of Stephen: "Godly men buried Stephen and mourned deeply for him" (Acts 8:2). In the next chapter of Acts, we read of widows grieving the death of Dorcas, a godly servant. As they wept over their loss, they also remembered her service to the church. Acts 9:39 describes the scene: "Peter went with them, and when he arrived he was taken upstairs to the room. All the widows stood around him, crying and showing him the robes and other clothing that Dorcas had made while she was still with them." Even Jesus, the Son of God, grieved the death of his good friend Lazarus. John 11:33–36 reads, "When Jesus saw [Mary] weeping, and the Jews who had come along with her also weeping, he was deeply moved in spirit and troubled. 'Where have you laid him?' he asked. 'Come and see, Lord,' they replied. Jesus wept. Then the Jews said, 'See how he loved him!'" The apostle Paul also grieved as he anticipated the death of Epaphroditus, a fellow worker in the Lord. He wrote to the church in Philippi, "Indeed he was ill, and almost died. But God had mercy on him, and not on him only but also on me, to spare me sorrow upon sorrow" (Philippians 2:27).

Grief is part of the human experience, a reflection of our being created in God's image. The Father grieved the wickedness of pre-flood humanity (Genesis 6:6); Jesus, the sinless Son of God, grieved (as noted above); and the Holy Spirit grieves when believers sin against one another (Ephesians 4:30). Because we live in a world marred by sin and death, we understand that death is not the way it is supposed to be. Made in God's image, we recognize that death is wrong. We are emotional creatures, and therefore we grieve this.

At the same time, however, the Bible teaches us that death has been defeated by the cross of Jesus Christ and his resurrection. Because of this, we can embrace grief. The Bible teaches us that *God delights in the death of a believer*. In Psalm 116:15, we read these words: "Precious in the sight of the LORD is the death of his faithful servants." Although death is a result of the curse of sin (Genesis 2:17) and is our final enemy (1 Corinthians 15:26), God does not ultimately view the death of a believer as a bad thing. Yes, it is painful, a stark reflection of the fact that the world is still not redeemed from the curse of sin. And yet God tells us that the death of those he loves is precious. John affirms this in Revelation 14:13: "Then I heard a voice from heaven say, 'Write this: Blessed are the dead who die in the Lord from now on!' 'Yes,' says the Spirit, 'they will rest from their labor, for their deeds will follow them.'"

When we hear that God considers the death of those he loves "precious" there are two questions that naturally arise. Why is the death of a believer precious to God? And why does the Bible present the death of a believer as a good and positive event when it is so painful to us? Let's look at how the Bible answers these important questions.

A Ministry of Comfort

The Scriptures teach that God delights in the death of a believer because such a death employs the ministry of God's comfort. In 2 Corinthians 1:3–7 we read these words:

> Praise be to the God and Father of our Lord Jesus Christ, the Father of compassion and the God of all comfort, who comforts us in all our troubles so that we can comfort those in any trouble with the comfort we ourselves receive from God. For just as we share abundantly in the sufferings of Christ, so also our comfort abounds through Christ. If we are distressed, it is for your comfort and salvation; if we are comforted, it is for your comfort, which produces in you patient endurance of the same sufferings we suffer. And our hope for you is firm, because we know that just as you share in our sufferings, so also you share in our comfort.

When we grieve, our attention should be intentionally drawn to God. This is what Paul means when he refers to God as "the Father of compassion and the God of all comfort." In other words, there is no compassion in this life that does not ultimately come from the Father. There is no comfort that does not ultimately come from God. He is the God of *all* comfort. And he comforts us *in* all our troubles; in the midst of our grief and pain, God comes to our aid. In suffering, we experience the comfort of God in a deeper way than could ever be experienced if our lives were free of anguish and affliction.

One of the reasons the Father comforts us is so we may, in turn, comfort others. Verse 4 declares that God comforts us "so that [here's the purpose] we can comfort those in any trouble with the comfort we ourselves receive from God." God comforts us in the midst of our troubles so we will be better equipped to comfort others. Some may think this is strange, but Paul addresses that. He writes, "For just as we share abundantly in the sufferings of Christ, so also our comfort abounds through Christ" (2 Corinthians 1:5). In other words, our capacity to receive comfort is connected to our experience of suffering and our awareness of our need for God's mercy and compassion. As we suffer with Jesus, we are also comforted with him.

Another Scripture that illustrates this principle is 1 Thessalonians 4:13–18. Here Paul teaches that the death of a believer employs God's comfort by reminding us of the return of Jesus Christ. First Thessalonians was written, in part, because the believers were confused about the timing of prophetic events. As Paul corrected their theology of the end times, he also brought God's comfort to them.

> We do not want you to be uninformed about those who sleep in death, so that you do not grieve like the rest of mankind, who have no hope [believers grieve, but they do so differently from unbelievers]. For we believe that Jesus died and rose again, and so we believe that God will bring with Jesus those who have fallen asleep in him. According to the Lord's word, we tell you that we who are still alive, who are left until the coming of the Lord, will certainly not precede those who have fallen asleep. For the Lord himself will come down from heaven, with a loud command, with the voice of the archangel and with the trumpet call of God, and the dead in Christ will rise first. After that, we who are still alive and are left will be caught up together with them in the clouds to meet the Lord in the air. And so we will be with

the Lord forever. Therefore *encourage one another with these words* [emphasis added].

The apostle makes it clear that he wrote to the church in Thessalonica to comfort believers who did not know what would happen to fellow believers who had already died. He helped them understand that "the dead in Christ will rise first." In other words, if we are alive on this earth when Jesus returns, then Christians like my friend Jean precede us. The resurrection of Jean's body will precede our being taken, but we will meet her in the air. Paul essentially says, "Don't worry about fellow believers who die. God will be faithful in caring for those who have died in Christ before us. They are secure in him. Be sure to encourage one another with these truths." The death of believers is an occasion to remember these wonderful theological truths—the promise of our resurrection and God's future care for those he loves, even those who have died.

A Ministry That Exalts Jesus and the Value of Knowing Him

A second reason the death of believers is precious to God is because it exalts the infinite value of knowing Jesus Christ. In Philippians 1:18–20, we read these words:

> I will continue to rejoice, for I know that through your prayers and God's provision of the Spirit of Jesus Christ what has happened to me [my imprisonment] will turn out for my deliverance. I eagerly expect and hope that I will in no way be ashamed, but will have sufficient courage so that now as always Christ will be exalted in my body, whether by life or by death.

Paul is convinced that he belongs to Jesus Christ and, therefore, his Lord will be exalted whether he lives or whether he dies. His classic statement "for to me, to live is Christ and to die is gain" (verse 21) verbalizes his conviction that to live is to know Christ, to walk with Christ, to be in fellowship with him, and to serve him. Paul says this is what it means to live. He is saying, "If I can't do that, then why live at all?" Paul saw his death as spiritual gain, not because death itself is good, but because he knew that, as frightening and painful as the process of dying can be, it is the vehicle to immediately bring him into the real presence of the Lord, whom he loved and served.

Paul continues in verses 22–24: "If I am to go on living in the body, this will mean fruitful labor for me. Yet what shall I choose? I do not know! I am torn between the two: I desire to depart and be with Christ, which is better by far; but it is more necessary for you that I remain in the body."

Paul felt like he was caught between a rock and a hard place. He loved Christ, and he loved serving him with his life. Yet he also knew that the moment he died, he would be with his Lord; he would gain his heart's deepest desire. Part of him wanted to stay on earth and serve Christ with all his heart, and part of him wanted to go to be with his Savior immediately. He knew that if his earthly life continued, it was to be for the sake of other believers.

As Christians, we need to have the same mind-set. Whatever time God gives us here should be used to serve others in his name. Rather than fear death, believers can keep their focus on what follows death, namely, being immediately present with the Lord we love.

Later in the same letter, Paul reveals his heart's passion: "I want to know Christ—yes, to know the power of his resurrection and participation in his sufferings, becoming like him in his death" (3:10). Paul was driven to know Christ, even if it required his own death. Paul knew that since death leads to the next stage of his relationship with the Savior, it is not the end. Death is a new beginning, where we live in the presence of the Savior who died for us and await our final resurrection. Being in the presence of the way and the truth and the life *is* life, not death. First John 3:2 testifies, "Dear friends, now we are children of God, and what we will be has not yet been made known. But we know that when Christ appears, we shall be like him, for we shall see him as he is." This is our hope! Seeing Jesus face-to-face will lead to our transformation and we shall be like him. Because this is true, we can rejoice, even in the midst of our grief.

A Ministry of Longing for Christ's Return

Finally, God delights in the death of a believer because it stirs anticipation for the fullness of redemption. The death of a believer builds in our hearts a longing for the redemption that is coming to us in Jesus and his return. The death of a believer produces a desire for the completion of what God has begun (Philippians 1:6). This is Paul's point in 2 Corinthians 5:1–8:

> We know that if the earthly tent we live in [the human body that houses who we really are] is destroyed, we have a building from God [the glorified body of the believer], an eternal house in heaven, not built by human hands. Meanwhile we groan, longing to be clothed instead with our heavenly dwelling, because when we are clothed, we will not be found

naked. For while we are in this tent, we groan and are burdened, because we do not wish to be unclothed but to be clothed instead with our heavenly dwelling, so that what is mortal may be swallowed up by life. Now the one who has fashioned us for this very purpose is God, who has given us the Spirit as a deposit, guaranteeing what is to come.

Therefore we are always confident and know that as long as we are at home in the body we are away from the Lord. For we live by faith, not by sight. We are confident, I say, and would prefer to be away from the body and at home with the Lord.

Here Paul looks forward to the fullness of his redemption. When he speaks of the earthly tent (the human body that is already in the process of decaying, even while we live), his heart is filled with anticipation. While we live here, in this fallen world, we groan and are burdened. Yet we know that the Holy Spirit has been given to us as a pledge, as a down payment, the promise of something more to come, which is the resurrection—at which time our mortal bodies will be "swallowed up by life" (verse 4). When our bodies are raised from the grave, we shall receive new ones—glorified bodies—that will not be susceptible to cancer, strokes, or heart disease. They will never die again. We will live with the Lord, whole and complete, for all eternity.

In the great resurrection chapter (1 Corinthians 15), Paul writes, "The last enemy to be destroyed is death" (verse 26). When Jesus rose from the grave on the first day of the week, he secured our resurrection. He is "the firstfruits of those who have fallen asleep" (verse 20), meaning that his resurrection is the guarantee of more resurrections still to come. At the final resurrection, Paul tells us that death will be forever destroyed. Until then, death is our enemy, and it seeks to threaten us and lead us to despair. Paul David Tripp writes this:

> We all feel death's wrenching finality. Death is so wrong, so completely out of step with life as God planned it. The apostle Paul could think of no better word for it than "enemy" (1 Corinthians 15:25–26). Death is the enemy of everything good and beautiful about life … Death was simply not meant to be. When you recognize this, you will hunger for the complete restoration of all things. You will long to live with the Lord in a place where the last enemy—death—has been defeated.[11]

The glorified bodies of believers will one day be rejoined with their spirits, which are now present with Christ. One day, body and soul together, we will spend eternity with the Lord in a new heaven and a new earth.

God uses the sorrow of death in his church to produce in us a hunger for all things to be restored, to the glory of Christ. Our hope as believers is not bound to the things of this world, not even to those we love the most. "Ours," writes Charles Spurgeon in a sermon titled "The Hope Laid Up in Heaven," "is a hope which demands nothing of time, or earth, but seeks its all in the world to come."[12] The death of a believer reminds us that we must live every day in light of the imminent return of Jesus our Lord when he will usher in the final restoration of all things.

Our grief is real, but it is not final. It leads to understanding, to growth, and to our transformation. The Bible doesn't discourage our sorrow, even when fellow believers are ushered into glory. We don't need to pretend we are happy when we feel deep sadness. We don't need to hide our grief. Lament is a normal part of our Christian experience. However, it is not the end, the final word. We are not left with just our tears. Rather, our sorrow has a purpose, namely, to lead us to seek for something more certain than this transient life. Our grief encourages us to seek the promises of the gospel as the anchor for our soul.

When our friend Jean Pitz died, our church experienced genuine sorrow. We grieved. But our tears fell on the pages of Scripture. In our sorrow, we sought comfort from the One who has conquered death and the grave!

CHAPTER 3

VISITING THE GRIEVING

Compassionate, Personal Care

"The righteous will answer him, 'Lord, when did we see you hungry and feed you, or thirsty and give you something to drink? When did we see you a stranger and invite you in, or needing clothes and clothe you? When did we see you sick or in prison and go to visit you?'

"The King will reply, 'Truly I tell you, whatever you did for one of the least of these brothers and sisters of mine, you did for me.'"

Matthew 25:37–40

THE COMPASSION OF JESUS is often demonstrated in small ways. It can be a drink of water to a thirsty person. A visit to a stranger who needs a friend or a listening ear. These are the simple acts of mercy and kindness that the King of heaven will one day reward. As a minister of God's grace and comfort, there are many practical ways you can assist in offering comfort to those who are grieving, as you bring spiritual food and drink to the soul that is hungry and thirsty for the Lord's refreshment.

The purpose of this chapter is to provide counsel concerning things to keep in mind when making contact with someone who has just lost a close friend or loved one. What do we need to be conscious of? How can we offer biblical hope and encouragement to those who are deeply hurting? These are the kinds of questions this chapter addresses. The focus here is on ways to show compassion when the loss is still very fresh. The chapter that follows this one will consider long-term bereavement care.

If there is one character quality, or posture of care, that we must model as servants of the Lord, it is *gentleness*. As the Lord's servants we are called to be kind and gentle to all, even to those who oppose us (2 Timothy 2:24–25). If this gracious posture is required of us, even toward our enemies, then how much more must we be careful to exhibit a gentle spirit and speak gentle words to those in our flock whose wounds of grief are still open and bleeding.

Gently Bring Them Comfort by Your Quiet Presence

Sadly, Job's counselors will forever be known as miserable comforters, for that is what they were when they sought only to blame Job for his trials, which included the deaths of his ten children. However, there is one thing these three men did right. Here's what the sacred text says (pay special attention to the last sentence):

> When Job's three friends, Eliphaz the Temanite, Bildad the Shuhite and Zophar the Naamathite, heard about all the troubles that had come upon him, they set out from their

homes and met together by agreement to go and sympathize with him and comfort him. When they saw him from a distance, they could hardly recognize him; they began to weep aloud, and they tore their robes and sprinkled dust on their heads. Then they sat on the ground with him for seven days and seven nights. No one said a word to him, because they saw how great his suffering was.

Job 2:11–13

The one thing these friends did right, which contributed to Job's comfort in his time of great trial, was to offer him their silent presence. I'm convinced we often fail to recognize how powerfully our quiet presence may minister to someone in the first hours and days of their deep valley of sorrow. When someone you love loses someone they love, it can be powerfully therapeutic to them (in the best sense of the word) to carefully close your mouth, open your ears, and perhaps even offer a tender touch if it is appropriate. As you care for those who are grieving, be sure to take time to truly mourn with those who mourn (Romans 12:15). Don't be too quick to offer answers. (This is especially true in the case of suicide.) Let them cry. Allow them the freedom to feel numb. Pray for them. And pray that you will speak wisely when the time is right. *Let them know you care by simply being there.*

Quiet presence is an important part of our ministry to one another in times of loss; however, it is not sufficient. At the appropriate time, we must gently speak words of grace and truth, and do so in love — for their comfort and the nurturing of their faith in Christ (Ephesians 4:15). Make sure your words are saturated with God's words, but not in a preachy manner or tone. Pursue gentleness (1 Timothy 6:11). There may come a time for stronger exhortation later down the road if you sense that their grief is becoming self-consuming and debilitating. However, even then, be careful that you speak for their benefit, not simply to make yourself feel better for getting something off your chest. Come alongside them with God's words of promise, comfort (2 Corinthians 1:3–4), and compassion (Colossians 3:12) in a timely manner (Ephesians 4:29). Aim to practice incarnational ministry—a ministry that models the mind-set of Jesus as you strive to be "full of [both] grace and truth" (John 1:14).

Gently Lead Them to the Good Shepherd

As important and necessary as our personal presence is to those who are grieving, ultimately it is the Lord's presence that will meet the deepest needs of the hurting soul. Knowing this, it is vital that we lead the members of our flock to think deliberately of the truth that Jesus is not only Lord and Savior but also the faithful good shepherd. One example of how to do this is to tie Psalm 23, "the LORD is my shepherd," with Jesus' description of himself—"I am the good shepherd" (John 10:11).

Read to them Psalm 23, gently reminding them of the Lord's care for his sheep. Especially draw their attention to the assurance of God's continued presence. The Lord does not leave us to suffer alone. No, he walks through the valley of the shadow of death *with us*! He comforts us in our times of grief by walking with us, holding our hand as we face indescribable pain.

Move from Psalm 23 to Jesus' words about being the good shepherd. Read to them John 10:11–15 and connect the dots. Explain that the promises found in Psalm 23 belong to those who have embraced Jesus. Those who belong to Christ not only receive great and precious promises for the life to come, but gracious assurances for life here on earth. When we know the good shepherd, Jesus, we may confidently say with David, "The LORD is *my* shepherd, I lack nothing" (Psalm 23:1).

Jesus, the good shepherd, has already laid down his life for them (verse 11). When Jesus first spoke the words, "The good shepherd lays down his life for the sheep," his sacrificial death was still in the future. But that work is now complete. His sin-bearing work is finished, and the sinner's debt is paid in full (John 19:30; Hebrews 9:27–28). By consciously remembering this past demonstration of Jesus' great love, the heart of the grieving believer is further assured of the Lord's continued love and care, now—each and every day—and to eternity.

Jesus, the good shepherd, will never act like a hired hand by leaving his sheep (verse 12). Instead, the faithful shepherd stays right by his sheep. He will never leave them; he will never abandon them in their grief (Hebrews 13:5). He will never leave them to wage war alone against the enemy of their soul.

Jesus, the good shepherd, is committed to and concerned for each of his sheep (verse 13). The hired hand flees because he is self-centered, but Jesus continues to lead, feed, and comfort his own. Why? Because Jesus' commitment to his sheep is contained not in empty words but in deep promises, like the promise to remain present in the dark valleys of life.

Jesus, the good shepherd, knows his sheep in relationship, just as he knows the Father in relationship (verses

14–15). Jesus knows those who are his own, and those who are his own know him. What a wonderful truth! Especially since Jesus in the next verse likens his relationship with us to his relationship with the Father, which has existed for eternity. Knowing Christ includes a deepening intimacy of relationship with the good shepherd. As we listen to his word and gently speak it to those who grieve, they will find comfort and security in the enduring love of God.

The good shepherd continues to love and care for those who trust him. When we set our minds on these truths and carefully minister gracious words, the grieving members of our flock will find their hearts resting securely in God's presence.

Gently Reassure Them That God Understands Their Pain

To effectively minister God's grace in times of loss, we must carefully reassure the grieving person of the comforting character of God and the compassion of Jesus. During the process of grieving, those who experience loss may need to be reminded that what they are going through is part of the human experience. But we need to be careful not to use clichés like, "We all go through hard times, but God will somehow bring good out of this."

Because the experience of loss is part of the human experience, we have opportunity to make wise use of the present reality to gently direct hurting people to biblical examples of grief and, most importantly, to the most "fully human" person who ever lived—Jesus. Biblical examples of grief teach us about the depth and reality of life's pain. Abraham grieved the loss of his wife, Sarah, as described in Genesis 23:2. Here the

Hebrew word *sapad* ("mourn") means "to tear the heart and beat the breast." The Hebrew word *bakah* ("weep") means "to lament with great sorrow." Understand the depth of sorrow that accompanies the loss of a close loved one. It is not something that a person gets over quickly or easily. Reassure them "the LORD is close to the brokenhearted" (Psalm 34:18).

Reflect on the compassion and sympathy of Christ, which produced tears over the loss of his friend Lazarus and the painful grief of his friend's family. In his classic essay "The Emotional Life of Our Lord," first published in 1912, theologian B. B. Warfield states that Jesus was not afraid of compassion's "manifestation in tears and sighs. The tears ... wet his cheeks." Warfield explains that Jesus' tears at the tomb of Lazarus (John 11:35) were "tears of sympathy ... The sight of suffering drew tears from his eyes; obstinate unbelief convulsed him with uncontrollable grief."[13] By turning the grieving person's eyes to Jesus, we give them permission to grieve, for Jesus grieved deeply, and yet he never sinned.

The person overwhelmed with sorrow needs to understand that grieving itself is not sin. It may lead to sin later down the road if their grief leads to bitterness or becomes an excuse to avoid responsibility and thus negatively affects the people around them. But corrective counsel for that situation is for another time, not now. Now is the time for gentle assurance, love, and patience.

Finally, pray with them, as you blend your comforting presence and your words of assurance that God understands their pain. Graciously lead them like a gentle shepherd. Draw them to the throne of grace, where God promises to give them mercy and grace in their time of need (Hebrews 4:15).

Gently Counsel and Comfort through the Use of Sympathy Cards

It is imperative that your immediate ministry of presence be followed shortly afterward with written words of encouragement, assurance of your continued prayers, and expressions of Christ-centered hope. My practice is to wait about one week after the funeral before sending a carefully written card to each grieving member of my flock. I have found that at the moment of death, it is my quiet, helpful presence that is needed most, not my words. As a local church shepherd, I will have the privilege of taking many opportunities in the months and years ahead to provide ongoing comfort.

One appropriate means is to use carefully selected sympathy cards. Avoid the use of generic cards that have no solid Christian message. Also, when the spiritual condition of the deceased is unknown, avoid sympathy cards that unquestionably usher the deceased into heaven. False hope provides no real, lasting comfort.

Since my mother's death, I have radically altered my use of sympathy cards, especially with regard to the words I write in them. I now know more fully the pain that death immediately brings into our lives, and after having received so many impactful words of comfort from others, I am convinced I will never write in a card the same way I did before. Carefully chosen words delivered God's compassion to our hearts in the days and weeks immediately following our loss.

Years later, these written expressions of love and care still minister to me. From these cards, I have drawn four characteristics of a good sympathy card. You might even consider them "gifts" that we give to those who are grieving. I offer them to you, along with examples of what other people wrote to my family, as suggestions to apply in order to become a more effective minister of comfort to those who grieve (2 Corinthians 1:4).

1. PERMISSION: Give them permission to grieve or be shocked. Use words that communicate freedom to experience and release pain, such as:

> The pain of your loss is greater when your heart has been touched deeply and your life affected more profoundly by the one you have loved.
>
> We are never prepared for the loss of a loved one, but God's grace and mercy are new every morning. He is faithful in times of grief and he, using both his Word and his children, will strengthen you in the days ahead.

2. HONESTY: If you don't know what to say, admit it. Don't feel pressured to come up with some profound words that don't represent the real you. Include brief Scripture quotations of comfort. Remember, the one thing Job's "comforters" did right is to sit with him for a week without saying a word (Job 2:13). Your unspoken presence will mean the world to those who grieve.

> If we knew what to say, we would not know how to say it. We are asking God to give grace running over as you and your family deal with this difficult hour.

3. EMPATHY: Show them understand without actually saying, "I understand what you are going through." For example, one man wrote these words:

Comfort the Grieving

I was deeply saddened to hear of your mother's death. I lost my own mother in a similarly unexpected way, and I well remember the sense of shock. I pray the comfort of the Spirit of Christ will be with you and your family, especially your little ones who will be without their grandmother at Christmas.

4. ASSISTANCE: Open your ears to listen to them, and your heart to serve them. Another brother in Christ wrote this:

My deepest sympathy to you in the passing of your mom! Having gone through this same trial two years ago, I understand and share your pain. I always thought the passing of an elderly parent would not be that hard. But I found out I was wrong; it is. Waves of emotions or memories wash over often when least expected. Trust me. It does get better with time. If you ever need a brother just to listen, feel free to call me any time. I am here for you.

If you do offer to help the grieving person in practical ways, be sure to specifically follow up with them later. Overwhelmed with grief and the common tendency to pull into the turtle's shell, so to speak, they probably will not call you. But if you call them and say, "Let's get a cup of coffee," they may be glad to accept. And when you go, be ready to listen and slow to speak (James 1:19).

CHAPTER 4

GRACE FOR THE JOURNEY

Long-Term Bereavement Care

The LORD ... heals the brokenhearted
and binds up their wounds.
Psalm 147:2–3

He tends his flock like a shepherd:
He gathers the lambs in his arms
and carries them close to his heart.
Isaiah 40:11

SHORTLY AFTER BEGINNING a new ministry, Pastor Kevin Ruffcorn stopped by to visit a young widow whose husband had died of a heart attack three years earlier. The widow quickly cut to the chase:

> The pastor and the church didn't minister to my greatest needs. Oh, the pastor saw me right after the death, and he met with me before the service. He said a few words at the funeral. But I never saw him again in regard to my husband's death. After the first week, no one from the congregation visited with us concerning our grief. My real struggles with my husband's death didn't begin until

two weeks after the funeral, and by then, everyone was out of sight.

Sadly, this is too often true. Ruffcorn comments, "The memorial service, I began to understand, wasn't the place to terminate ministry [to the bereaved]. It was the place to begin a different but no less important one."[14] Ministering to those who have lost a loved one is a unique privilege and responsibility, and one that requires long-term attention.

Support for those experiencing loss needs to extend far beyond the traditional sympathy card to include phone calls, visits, and Christian fellowship over meals. We must intentionally help those who grieve to adjust to the reality of the changes that have shaken their world.

It is impossible to overemphasize the importance of getting members of the church family involved in comforting one another. The bereaved need to be encouraged to "stay connected." Paul David Tripp counsels the grieving person, "God likens the church to a physical body of interconnected and interdependent parts. He reminds us that life is a community project. In grief, it is tempting to turn inside yourself and avoid the community around you."[15] Therefore, pastors must gently urge those who are grieving to resist the temptation to pull away and instead to remain as involved as possible in the body life of the church. But they need more than gentle nudging; they need their shepherds to remain attentive to their need for ongoing care and counsel.

This chapter simply reflects my own attempt to be available for the grieving members of my flock. I have made my share of mistakes as a pastor, but God is gracious to continue to help me become more faithful as an undershepherd of his flock.

In this chapter, I provide practical helps that may also encourage your growth as a fellow minister of the gospel. Here you will hear a call for extended ministry to the bereaved, including a suggested plan for sixteen months of follow-up care, which activates members of the body of Christ to serve one another with compassion. The biblical analogy between the church and the human body has numerous implications for grief ministry. Since when "one part suffers, every part suffers with it" (1 Corinthians 12:26), no one in the church should have to walk through their darkest valleys alone — ever!

Sixteen-Month to Three-Year Bereavement Care

Early in my tenure as a pastor, I had the privilege of serving as a volunteer chaplain for a local hospice. Impressed by the length of time the nursing staff devoted to following up with the family of the deceased, I began to see the need for long-term bereavement care in the church. Since that time, I have sought to be more intentional as a shepherd in continuing to care for the bereaved long after the memorial service has ended, the flowers have wilted, the phone has gone silent, and the mail carrier has stopped delivering cards and letters.

The following chart is an example of a plan designed to comfort and encourage a widower in my church and his extended family. Every minister of God's grace should come up with his own plan, which will vary from person to person and change along the way. The details of our approaches will differ, but an intentional plan will prevent the bereaved from being forgotten by church leaders and members, or from slipping through the cracks of a busy ministry. Notice how the care begins on a weekly basis, primarily from a pastor, and gradually transitions to monthly care provided by others in the church but still remaining under the oversight of a church shepherd, who is called to be an overseer of God's flock.

Week following the death	Personal Contact	Primary caregiver
Week 1	Take widower to lunch. Send sympathy cards to all relatives in the church. Include copies of comforting hymn lyrics inside the cards. Give the widower an appropriate sermon CD, such as "God's Delight in the Death of a Believer."	Pastor
Week 2	Phone call. Written copies of funeral sermon to all family members, if deemed appropriate.	Pastor
Week 3	Lunch	Pastor
Week 4	Send "Praying for you" cards to family members. Try to remember key holidays that will be especially difficult during the first year following the death, such as the birthday of the deceased, Mother's Day, wedding anniversary, etc. Put reminders on your computer or in your diary.	Pastor
Week 5	Lunch	Man in church
Week 6	Give widower a small booklet to read, such as *Heaven* by Jonathan Edwards. If the bereaved person is ready for a bigger book, I highly recommend *Sunsets: Reflections for Life's Final Journey* by Deborah Howard. If the deceased is a child, I highly recommend *From Grief to Glory* by James Bruce (resources listed in appendix 4).	Pastor

Week 7	Phone call	Deacon
Week 8	Send a list of comforting Scriptures.	Pastor
Week 10	Lunch	Deacon and others
Week 12	Give him a booklet such as *Grief: Finding Hope Again* by Paul David Tripp.	Pastor
Week 14	Phone call	Man in church
Week 16	Invite him to your house for a light snack after Sunday evening service, with a few others from church.	Pastor, deacon, or another family in the church
Months 5–11	Have some form of personal contact at least once a month. Be creative.	Involve as many others in the church family as possible.
One Year: anniversary of death	This will be a hard day for most people. They will need some form of personal contact: a hand to hold, a hug, some type of physical contact. They need reassurance of how God has faithfully brought them through the past year.	Pastor should ask a friend of the bereaved to provide this encouragement.
Months 13–15	Have some form of personal contact at least once a month. Be creative.	Involve as many others in the church as possible.
Month 16	Lunch	Pastor and deacon

Ministering to two women who were widowed taught me that some need attentive care for a longer time. Therefore, cards and intentional pastoral contact continue for some.

Others do not need this care. One woman asked me to stop sending cards since they caused grief to resurface for her. Each pastor will need to discern where each bereaved person is in their own journey of grief.

When the primary griever is a woman, the minister who is married is encouraged to have his wife accompany him when making visits. The unmarried pastor should take along two other church members (ideally a mature couple) in order to avoid sending an improper message or putting any temptation in front of the bereaved, or himself. This will also immediately give the grieving woman additional connections in the church family.

In keeping with the Titus 2:3–5 philosophy of ministry, church shepherds, married and unmarried alike, should get other spiritually mature women in the church involved as soon as possible and transition the personal care to them while remaining available to provide counsel to the primary caregivers. Teaching shepherds should always equip their sheep to care for one another in the flock. The experience of grief in a local church becomes a time to test how effectively believers have been, and are being, prepared to serve one another. The faithful pastor who diligently equips his church members for ministry will be pleasantly surprised and deeply fulfilled by the initiative these servants show in times of loss.

In the particular case of the widower, much more one-another ministry was carried out spontaneously by other members of the church body. For example, numerous families invited the bereaved families over for a meal, and a number of men had lunch with the widower. The pastor will do his flock much good by constantly teaching other-member care and the practice of biblical fellowship in the church. It is a delight to watch a well-trained body function as God designed.

In his chapter in *Suffering and the Sovereignty of God*, Dustin Shramek provides this plain counsel: "We love them by first weeping with them."[16] This simple description of comforting those who grieve is consistent with the biblical admonition to "rejoice with those who rejoice; mourn with those who mourn" (Romans 12:15). The familial bonds in the church, the family of God, demand that we care for one another in times of grief and pain. Deborah Howard writes the following:

> What can we do to help those experiencing grief? First we must be where we can see the problem — in contact with those we suspect are hurting. One of the most important things we can do is just to be there. Our presence speaks louder than words. There are two things we need to take them every time we go — hope and a tender, listening heart. We don't have to come up with flowery phrases. Sitting quietly with them is more comforting than preaching sermons to them. And sometimes we can gently direct their thinking toward the faithfulness of God.[17]

Counseling Those Dealing with Death and Loss

Comforting those who grieve includes appropriately counseling them to apply biblical truth and principles that are necessary for their spiritual health and joyful living. Reading the Scriptures, especially the book of Psalms, brings us back to the reality of what life in a fallen world looks and feels like. Sorrow, which even leads to depression at times, is common in the human experience. Therefore, we must know how to help others navigate through their "valley times" with the Lord. In order to come alongside the grieving and help them strive for biblical joy, I have summarized the kind of counsel we need to provide with the following four "R's":

Refresh

Those who have experienced grief and loss need to remember God's design for healthy living, which includes adequate rest and refreshment for the body and spirit. In other words, if God is mindful that "we are dust" (Psalm 103:14), then we need to remember that as well. It is not uncommon for grieving people to neglect their daily needs. Though less important than the pursuit of godliness, the proper care of our body is of some profit (1 Timothy 4:8) and will have a profound impact on the condition of one's spirit.

Music marks the significant moments in life — times of joy and sorrow — and plays an important role in many of life's celebrations. But nothing matches its ability to touch the deepest parts of our inner person and provide spiritual and mental refreshment in the midst of our grief and pain. The most vivid biblical example of the power of music to minister to the inner man is the effect that David's music had on King Saul. In 1 Samuel 16:23, we read, "Whenever the spirit from God came on Saul, David would take up his lyre and play. Then relief would come to Saul; he would feel better, and the evil spirit would leave him." The music itself ministered to the king, helping him in his pain and causing him to feel refreshed.

Spiritual songs and great hymns of the faith, which wed biblical truths to memorable melodies, are powerful refreshment to the soul. Music makes the promises of God resonate in people's souls in a unique and beautiful way. For this reason, I often insert a photocopy of a hymn into the cards I send during our long-term bereavement care.

Remain

The grieving believer will often need gentle reminders to abide in Christ by remaining in fellowship with God and his people through the practice of spiritual disciplines: spending time in God's word, praying, connecting with God's people, and nurturing close friendships.

1. Remain in God's word. By doing so, the grieving soul speaks truth into his or her heart, which naturally believes its own lies. It is important for a person in deep sorrow to be honest with their emotions and wrestle through them biblically. Scriptures that model this process include Psalms 42; 55; 73; and 77. Another precious, soul-feeding study is the comparison of the shepherd of Psalm 23 with the good shepherd of John 10, as mentioned in chapter 3.

2. Remain in prayer. Souls that are overcome with grief must choose to discipline themselves to cast their cares on the Lord, through prayer, while knowing and choosing to believe the heavenly Father truly cares for them. Praying Psalms 42 and 43, for example, is one way to remain in communion with God, especially when emotions are less than supportive. The grieving person needs to be encouraged to not be ashamed when their own resources are depleted and they need to "borrow" from a brother or sister in Christ by reading God's word with them and praying together.

3. Remain in fellowship with God's people. God has graciously provided a means by which his people receive their necessary comfort and encouragement — the local church, the family of God. Without apology, the writer of Hebrews identifies one of the purposes of the fellowship of Christians as "encouraging one another" (Hebrews 10:25). Too often we forget that the word *encourage* means "to give courage." The grieving soul lacks courage and therefore needs to get courage from other believers by remaining in fellowship with them. In his book on grief ministry, *God's Healing for Life's Losses*, Bob Kellemen counsels the grieving with these appropriate, direct words: "Grief tempts us to walk alone. Fight that temptation. Walk with God and His people as you journey on the healing path."[18]

4. Remain in friendship with faithful brothers or sisters in Christ. As I already mentioned, those who are grieving must consciously resist the tendency toward isolation, toward holing up and licking one's wounds. Though times of aloneness with God are necessary to the God-centered encouragement and feeding of the soul in sorrow, those times must not be divorced from intentional interaction with other believers they can trust and lean on. The friendship of David and Jonathan is perhaps the most treasured in the Bible. Their souls were knit together, and they loved each other as they loved their own lives (1 Samuel 18:1; 20:17). Surely this friendship was a great source of help to David on his saddest days!

Remember

Those who are grieving also need to be encouraged to discipline themselves to remember the Lord's works of mercy, love, and grace. The psalmist exhorts us to "forget not all his benefits" (Psalm 103:2). When we forget, it's most often because we do not choose to remember. One example of learning how to practice remembrance is to encourage the grieving to meditate on Scripture and journal the blessings of the Lord. Psalm

103 is a great place to begin. When I meditated on this psalm, it did not take me long to find no less than nineteen of the Lord's benefits toward me.

Review

Finally, the person who is filled with sorrow because of death and loss needs to review truths about God that we find in God's word. The writer of Psalms 42 and 43 did this as he talked to himself instead of letting his self talk to him. Again, journaling can be extremely beneficial here, since the grieving person is able to flip through the pages of the journal and be reminded of God's character and gracious works, and think about the times the Lord has helped him. The grieving person should be encouraged to begin a "Works of God" journal to record his gracious deeds toward them, no matter how small.

Another helpful journaling practice is to begin a "My God Is ..." list, recording the characteristics and attributes of God they encounter in their Scripture reading. Returning to these lists will serve them in the years ahead, whenever grief threatens to hover over their heart as a dark shadow. Biblical, positive thinking does not come naturally for any of us. We must discipline our mind to dwell not on our losses but on things that are true, noble, right, pure, lovely, admirable, excellent, and praiseworthy (Philippians 4:8).

Overcoming grief is not an overnight event. It is a process that takes time, sometimes many years. Let us, therefore, be mindful of the long-term bereavement care that God's people need from us, their shepherds.

CHAPTER 5

COMFORT THROUGH WRITING

The Art of Writing Hope-Dispensing Letters

> Writing is not only a process of communicating with yourself as well as with others but also a way of becoming more sensitive to other human beings.
>
> George P. Schultz

THE ART OF LETTER WRITING has virtually disappeared in this age of email and text messaging. Who can deny the sense of love that we feel when we receive a handwritten letter from a caring friend? To know that our need was important enough to that person that they set aside the time to write a good letter is encouraging in and of itself. The process of writing a letter also benefits the writer, as it clarifies the thinking process. To take the thoughts that float around in our heads and skillfully arrange them on paper is a discipline that greatly improves our understanding of ourselves and what we really believe about God, and it trains us to be "more sensitive to other human beings," as we are forced to consider how each word may affect them.

In his foreword to the *New York Times* bestseller *Reagan*, former secretary of state George Schultz says more about this discipline: "Anyone who writes knows what an effort it is to assemble your thoughts and commit them to a piece of paper. Writing is an exercise in communicating with yourself as well as with others. A good writer is almost of necessity a good thinker."[19] As pastors, the process of letter writing forces us to think through the issues that have a deep impact on members of our flock who are in the midst of suffering. As we do so, it makes us more sensitive shepherds. In addition to promoting our personal growth as pastors, much lasting ministry takes place through the writing of letters, as theological truths are communicated in a personal way, which can then be read over and over again.

An Example of a Hope-Dispensing Letter

As those who serve God's people in times of loss, pastors need to consider making the discipline of letter writing a regular part of their ministry of comfort. It is a very effective means of teaching Scripture and helping others apply its truth to life. The following is one example of this kind of letter.

> Dear brother,
>
> My heart has been aching with yours since I received the phone call about your father's death, preceded only a few weeks by your mother's. Then I think of the upheaval in your life since you suffered a stroke only six months ago. There's a reason that the familiar saying "when it

rains, it pours" is familiar. How true it is sometimes with God's sovereign timing of the life-changing events in our little worlds! I want you to know that I appreciate your testimony of faith in Christ and your simple trust in God during this painful time.

I've been thinking much this past week about why God ordains that these kinds of "tornadoes" pass through our lives. I want to encourage you with some biblical principles that have been simmering on the back burner of my mind. They come from two passages of Scripture. The first is Romans 8:28–29: "We know that in all things God works for the good of those who love him, who have been called according to his purpose. For those God foreknew he also predestined to be conformed to the image of his Son, that he might be the firstborn among many brothers and sisters."

In this portion of God's word, we see three incredible truths that apply to your current situation.

1. All things, even bad things, are used by God to accomplish good in the lives of believers. As a believer in Jesus Christ, you can know without a doubt that God is working out his good purpose in your life right at this moment—even if you cannot yet see it.

2. It is God who is at work in all things for your good. It is not merely a "things will work out in the end" or "whatever is meant to be is meant to be" kind of fatalism. But *God is actively at work* in your life right now through this trial.

3. The ultimate good that God is working all things in your life toward is that of shaping you into the image of Christ. Everything that God brings into our lives is for the ultimate purpose of his glory and our good. And the best "good" for us is that we become more like Jesus. Therefore, one of the most helpful questions you can ask right now is, "Lord, how can I become more like you because of these trials?"

The second Scripture passage is 2 Corinthians 1:2–5: "Grace and peace to you from God our Father and the Lord Jesus Christ. Praise be to the God and Father of our Lord Jesus Christ, the Father of compassion and the God of all comfort, who comforts us in all our troubles, so that we can comfort those in any trouble with the comfort we ourselves receive from God. For just as we share abundantly in the sufferings of Christ, so also our comfort abounds through Christ."

In this passage are five additional truths that will encourage your growth in Christ during and after your time of suffering.

1. Grace and peace come only from God and your Lord, Jesus Christ. Grace in time of need and an inner peace that enables you to reflect Christ in your time of trial are two of the infinite resources that are yours in Christ. With the loss of employment due to your stroke-induced disability, you can also be confident that God will provide your every material need: "My God will meet all your needs according to the riches of his glory in Christ Jesus" (Philippians 4:19).

2. God is "the Father of compassion and the God of all comfort." God sees you in your present suffering through his eyes of mercy and is ready to dispense divine comfort at every moment you need it. Indeed, he "comforts us in all our troubles."

3. Suffering expands our ministry. One significant reason that God comforts us in our troubles is so we can comfort others who are experiencing trials. This truth greatly encouraged my wife and me when we struggled with the news of our daughter's deafness. We often wonder who God will bring into our lives as a result of three of our children being hearing impaired. The same principle applies to you. There is no doubt in my mind that God is right now equipping you for future opportunities when others are afflicted in a similar way. What a joy it will be for you to be used by God in this way! We are all "comforters in training."

4. Suffering authenticates our ministry. Not only does suffering open the door to reaching more people with the hope of the gospel, but it also makes our own message of comfort more real — more believable — to those to whom we minister. We comfort others "with the comfort we ourselves receive from God." In other words, as in a relay race, we pass on to the next sufferer the same comfort that God has given to us.

5. Both suffering and comfort are abundant in the God-centered life. Just as Job asked his grieving wife, so we must say with contentment, "Shall we accept good from God, and not trouble?" (Job 2:10). Surely we must accept both. Increasingly, as we are conformed to the image of Christ, we will be able to accept both blessing and trial with the same gratitude and faith.

Again, I appreciate your trust in the Lord, brother, and I will continue to pray that God will use the promises in his precious Word to strengthen you in the inner man and enable you to reflect the glory of Christ to all those with whom you come into contact.

Your servant,
Pastor Paul

Comfort through Writing

Now, you may be asking why I chose the Scriptures and said some of the things I did in my letter. Let me explain. First, my desire was to encourage this man because I know from personal experience the temptation we all face when deluged by more than one major trial simultaneously—to get deeply discouraged and to lose hope. Therefore, I sought to direct his mind to truth about God that reassured him that God was for him, not against him; that he was called according to God's purpose and God was up to something good in all of his suffering.

Second, I wanted to establish him on the bedrock of God's sovereignty. When life seems to be falling apart, the sovereignty of God is an anchor to tie ourselves to and a rock to firmly plant our faith on. The passage from Romans 8 effectively accomplishes this. Furthermore, a well-established faith is what the apostle Paul desired for the Colossian believers—specifically, that they would stand firm and be rooted and built up in Christ (Colossians 1:23; 2:7).

Third, my desire was to help him look at his suffering through the lens of sanctification. Whatever our trial, there is one thing every believer in Christ may be fully assured of at all times—that our suffering is part of the means by which our heavenly Father is lovingly shaping us into the image of his Son, renewing us into the likeness of Christ (Romans 8:29; Colossians 3:10). When we learn to view trials through this lens, we move from asking *why* to asking *what*: What do you want me to learn in this time of trial, Lord? In what ways do I need to learn to trust you?

Fourth, I wanted to mentally prepare him to minister to

others somewhere down the road. I did this by reminding him that "the God of all comfort" brings his healing balm to us in order to equip us to be instruments of healing in other people's lives, to pass on the comfort we have received from him.

Finally, it was my desire to apply particular Scriptures to my suffering brother's situation to help train his mind to think biblically. Why? Because nothing tempts us to live by our emotions quite like unexpected trials and deep suffering. Therefore, I did not vaguely refer to Scripture in my letter, but quoted portions of the sacred text for him so he could easily follow its logic. I knew that ultimately it is God's words, not mine, that can strengthen him in the inner man.

In this case, the letter was prompted by the occasion of this man's stroke and the resulting unemployment, which took place not long after two significant losses. However, the biblical truths I pointed him to also apply to almost every form that suffering may take. Serving as God's undershepherds, we should strive to write letters that follow the model established by King Solomon, so that we are led by the Holy Spirit to write "words of the wise ... [that are] like firmly embedded nails— given by one shepherd" (Ecclesiastes 12:11).

Practical Advice for Busy Pastors

Most pastors are extremely busy preparing sermons and providing 24/7, on-call care for their flock. Therefore, the task of writing letters to individual members often falls by the wayside. Thus, establishing the habit of letter writing as part of your pastoral ministry will require personal discipline. This discipline entails simple organization and data collecting, as well as simply making time in one's schedule.

Comfort through Writing

1. Create a "life's major changes" database. I was able to put into practice the long-term bereavement care explained in chapter 4 by creating a simple plan for record keeping as part of our church membership database. A widow in our church provided many voluntary hours of data entry to set up the database, but keeping it current is a relatively simple task. Since our database already included wedding anniversaries and birthdays, the information we collected were the dates of the deaths of significant family members (spouse, parent, grandparent, and child) in the past three years. Having officiated at most of these funerals, I had much of the information already in my personal files. Whatever data I did not have was carefully and gently collected by my volunteer, who sensed a desire to be involved in grief ministry at the same time I was concluding that a record-keeping system was something I could no longer function without. The database allows us to print monthly reports related to the deceased and his or her family members (anniversary of death, wedding anniversary, and the deceased's birthday), thus enabling me to send them an appropriate card of comfort and encouragement.

2. Make letter writing a weekly habit. Monday became my normal letter-writing day. Since the personal interactions of Sunday were still on my mind and our pastoral team often spent time praying through the church directory on Monday, it was typical for at least three to six names to immediately pop into my head as those who could use a pastoral note of encouragement or a "Praying for You" card. These weekly pastoral letters were intended to direct the attention of God's sheep toward the good shepherd—and they were in addition to the cards sent out as part of the ongoing grief ministry mentioned earlier.

The Power of the New Testament Letters

The writing of letters that are pastoral in nature and tone is not new; much of the New Testament is comprised of such letters. In particular, the apostle Paul wrote his letters for the purpose of comforting the believers and reminding them of the hope that is theirs in Christ. He confidently assured the Corinthians of his firmly grounded hope for them and the comfort they shared in Christ (2 Corinthians 1:7). He encouraged the believers in the cities of Philippi and Colossae by informing them that he prayed for them constantly (Philippians 1:3), assuring them of his prayers for their spiritual well-being, that God would "fill [them] with the knowledge of his will through all the wisdom and understanding that the Spirit gives," in order that they may live a life worthy of the Lord, abundantly bear fruit in every good work, increase in true knowledge, experience God's strength, and endure life's trials with much patience (Colossians 1:9–12). In his first letter to the Thessalonian disciples, the apostle wrote words of doctrinal clarity for the purpose of comforting them, and he included in his second letter to them this rich, hope-dispensing benediction: "May our Lord Jesus Christ himself and God our Father, who loved us and by his grace gave us eternal encouragement and good hope, encourage your hearts and strengthen you in every good deed and word" (2 Thessalonians 2:16–17).

One of the obvious benefits of written words of comfort, hope, and encouragement is that they may be read over and over again, just as we are still reading the apostle's letters. Another widow in our church recently sent a card in which she thanked me for the many cards and letters she had received from me since her husband's death over five years ago. She made a point of telling me that she has kept every one of them and that they continue to bring comfort to her heart on days when her husband's absence is still acutely felt.

Clearly, the benefit of letters of hope that are carefully filled with Scripture and loving assurances of prayer cannot be overemphasized. The lost art of letter writing as a part of pastoral ministry needs to be recovered in our day. May the Lord bless and strengthen his church as we, his undershepherds, apply diligence in this often-neglected area of pastoral care!

PART 2

PREACHING THAT COMFORTS

"I LOVE TO PREACH AT FUNERALS." More than once after speaking these words, I have received odd looks from people. They think I'm morbid, obsessed with death. Though I admit I am often melancholy, I'm not morbid. And yet I really do love preaching at funerals. My love for preaching during these times is not due to a love for death itself, nor is it due to a strange enjoyment of grief and pain. No, I love to preach at funerals because they are unique, God-ordained opportunities to minister to people at a deeply significant time in their lives.

There are two reasons this is true. First, nothing is more radically intrusive than death. It puts everything else in life on hold. The day-to-day events and plans of life pause for a time—or, at the very least, our perspective changes as we look at our life. A funeral is a natural time for us to serve others because they need help and comfort and are aware of their need. It is often easier to serve people who sense their need to be served. They more readily receive our help.

Second, because nothing is more radically intrusive than death, a funeral is an ideal time to talk about life and death and what comes afterward. This needs to be done carefully and sensitively, but it should not be avoided. Because of this, funerals provide a fitting platform for evangelistic preaching.

The chapters in this section of the book contain sermons I have preached at various memorial services. Each message strives for clarity, simplicity, and sensitivity to the pain of grief, combined with a gentle, yet bold confrontation with the gospel. One of these messages is tailored for the grieving parents of a stillborn boy, the first of many pregnancies to go full-term. All three sermons are intentionally evangelistic. Each message assumes that more than a few people in the congregation lack biblical knowledge, so "the basics" are always covered, yet not in a dumbed-down fashion. Not only are unbelievers confronted with God's command to believe the gospel, but believers are drawn back to the purity of simple devotion to Jesus.

CHAPTER 6

Sermon 1
LIFE OUT
OF DEATH

> Christ also suffered once for sins, the righteous for the unrighteous, to bring you to God. He was put to death in the body but made alive in the Spirit.
>
> 1 Peter 3:18

FEW THINGS ARE MORE EFFECTIVE than a funeral for reminding us that life is temporary. The purpose of a memorial service is to honor one whose earthly life has come to an end. Death is often viewed as the end. But that is not really the truth. Death will teach us differently, if we stop long enough to listen. The death of a loved one can be a time for honest reflection on our own life, if we open our hearts to its message.

The central message of the Bible is a message of hope—that the death of one can bring life to many. You may ask, "How is that possible? How can death possibly bring about life? All that I see in death are sadness and grief. What good can come out of something as painful and difficult as death?"

One verse from God's word will help us answer that question. First Peter 3:18 reads, "Christ also suffered once for sins, the righteous for the unrighteous, to bring you to God. He was put to death in the body but made alive in the Spirit." This verse communicates an amazing truth—that God brings life out of death—and it tells us how God does this. God brings life out of the death of his only Son, Jesus Christ. In this short verse from 1 Peter, we see the Son of God described in three ways.

1. Christ Is Our Sacrifice

First, we see Jesus Christ as our sacrifice: "Christ also suffered once for sins." The first three chapters of the Bible tell us why there is death and where it came from. We learn that God created man from the dust of the earth and breathed into him the breath of life. Death was not God's original intention. We were made by our Creator to enjoy life—and to enjoy it with him. As creatures made in the image of God, man and woman enjoyed a unique relationship. This included intimate fellowship with their Creator. God told them their close relationship would continue as long as they remained obedient to his command not to eat from a certain tree in the garden. If they disobeyed God, there would be consequences. God warned them that they would surely die. Rather than obeying God and remaining in this special relationship with him, the man and woman chose to rebel against his authority. And just as God had said it would be, death was the result. Immediately, the couple experienced spiritual death. They knew they were no longer at peace with God, and they hid from his presence. Physical death followed their spiritual death. Eventually, Adam and Eve and all those descended from them would die. Their bodies would fail and succumb to old age or sickness, or they would experience death at the hands of sinful people or from the natural effects of a cursed world.

Immediately after their sin, God gave his disobedient people a sign of hope. God killed a lesser creature, an animal, and made clothing out of the skins. This was the first indication that God would accept a substitutionary sacrifice, that the death of one could "cover" the sins of another. We see this theme repeated again and again in the Bible.

Later in biblical history, God commanded a man named Abraham, the father of the Jewish nation, to offer his son as a sacrifice in order to test the loyalty of his love. We read the story in Genesis 22. Abraham trusted that God had the power to raise his son from death, so he obeyed, but before the knife was plunged into the boy's chest, God provided a ram to be offered as a sacrifice in place of Isaac.

Several hundred years later, during the time of Moses, God delivered his people from Egyptian bondage. After bringing several plagues on the Egyptians, God instructed his people that a final plague of death would come. To protect his people, God commanded each household to kill a lamb and sprinkle its blood on the doorposts of the house. Where no blood was seen by the Lord, the firstborn in that house would die. Yet if the Lord saw blood, he would pass over the house, leaving the firstborn alive. God's people were saved through the sacrifice of a lamb. God would eventually establish a formal sacrificial system so his people's sins could be forgiven based on the death of an animal.

Why does this matter? Because understanding the historical

and cultural background helps us understand what John the Baptist meant when he first saw Jesus. John exclaimed: "Look, the Lamb of God, who takes away the sin of the world!" (John 1:29). The Bible refers to Jesus as the "Lamb of God" because he was sent by God to be the ultimate sacrifice for sin — to give his life so that men and women might live and be delivered from the curse of sin and death. As Jesus hung on the cross, he took the penalty of our sin on himself, becoming our sacrifice and our Savior. His death now brings us life.

2. Christ Is Our Substitute

Second, the verse from 1 Peter indicates that Jesus Christ is our substitute: "Christ also suffered once for sins, *the righteous for the unrighteous*." God is holy. This means he is perfectly moral and just and cannot tolerate the presence of sin. His very nature requires that justice be done. But as we have seen, he will accept a sacrifice for sin. Since we are unjust, our sacrifice is unacceptable. We cannot right our own wrongs; we cannot make up for our sin. In our great need, the perfect Son of God became a man. And being man, he could die in man's place as our substitute. Being God's sinless Son, he is the *perfect* sacrifice, acceptable to God the Father. Because of this, a wondrous exchange takes place the moment a person turns from his or her sin to trust in Christ for salvation. The apostle Paul writes, "God made him who had no sin to be sin for us, so that in him we might become the righteousness of God" (2 Corinthians 5:21). As the sinner's substitute, Christ allowed the weight of man's guilt to be placed on him on the cross. God the Father then poured out his righteous wrath on his Son, punishing our sin once and for all (Hebrews 7:27). Jesus died *as if* he was guilty, though he was not.

There is another side to this exchange. When we as sinners turn to Christ in repentant faith, God credits the righteousness of Christ to our spiritual bank account and declares us righteous. We are justified in his sight, not by our own works or attempts to please God, but by faith in the One who took our punishment for us. In Galatians 2:15–16, Paul writes these words:

> We who are Jews by birth and not sinful Gentiles know that a person is not justified by the works of the law, but by faith in Christ Jesus. So we, too, have put out faith in Christ Jesus that we may be justified by faith in Christ and not by the works of the law, because by the works of the law no one will be justified.

Jesus Christ died to satisfy God's justice and give us life by taking away our sin and gifting us with his righteousness.

His death now brings us life.

3. Christ Is Our Savior

Third, Jesus Christ is our Savior. "Christ also suffered once for sins, the righteous for the unrighteous, to *bring you to God*." God's purpose in sending his Son was to satisfy his righteousness and justly deal with man's sin, as we have seen. And God accomplished this through the sinless life and atoning death of Jesus. The sacrifice of Christ as our substitute now provides a way for our broken relationship with God to be restored. John, one of Jesus' close followers, says it this way:

Comfort the Grieving

God so loved the world that he gave his one and only Son, that whoever believes in him shall not perish but have eternal life. For God did not send his Son into the world to condemn the world, but to save the world through him. Whoever believes in him is not condemned, but whoever does not believe stands condemned already because they have not believed in the name of God's one and only Son.

John 3:16–18

God has provided salvation for us through his Son, Jesus Christ. If you will come to him by faith, you will be forgiven and will receive his gift of eternal life. He who is *the* Savior will become *your* Savior. But the opposite is true as well. All who reject God's offer of salvation stand condemned and will only see God's face in the final judgment—not the face of a loving Father, but the face of a just Judge.

We must remember that death is not the end.

For some, death is the beginning of eternity apart from God because they refused to turn from their sin and instead rejected the giver of life—their sacrifice, substitute, and Savior. Jesus says in John 14:6, "I am the way and the truth and the life. No one comes to the Father except through me."

Yet for others, death is the beginning of eternity, an eternity spent in the presence of God because their trust was in the person and work of Jesus Christ alone. God brings life out of death.

What will death be for you?

CHAPTER 7

Sermon 2

OUR NEED FOR RECONCILIATION

Just as people are destined to die once,
and after that to face judgment ...

Hebrews 9:27

DEATH CAUSES PEOPLE TO ASK QUESTIONS about life.
"Why are we here?" "How do we make sense of such a short
life?" It all seems to make no sense. The Lord Jesus Christ
answers this question in Matthew 22:34–40:

> Hearing that Jesus had silenced the Sadducees, the Phari-
> sees got together. One of them, an expert in the law, tested
> him with this question: "Teacher, which is the greatest com-
> mandment in the Law?"
>
> Jesus replied: "'Love the Lord your God with all your
> heart and with all your soul and with all your mind.' This
> is the first and greatest commandment. And the second is
> like it: 'Love your neighbor as yourself.' All the Law and the
> Prophets hang on these two commandments."

Why Are We Here?

Quite simply, we are here to love God. We're designed to love God with such intensity that it spills over into love for our neighbors. Today, it is often said, "In order to truly love others, you must learn to love yourself." However, Jesus taught something radically different. He taught and lived a life that opposed every shade of self-centeredness, self-esteem, and self-love. He said in effect, "In order to truly love others, you must love God supremely."

According to the Bible, love is a response. We cannot love God until we have first responded to his love. First John 4:19 reads, "We love because he first loved us." How, then, do we respond to the love of God? In John's gospel, we read, "God so loved the world that he gave his one and only Son, that whoever believes in him shall not perish but have eternal life." Faith is the appropriate response to God's love. Faith receives and accepts the love of God offered in Jesus Christ.

Why did God send Christ? To meet man's greatest need. Man's greatest need is not to achieve world peace, to promote better health care, or to save the environment. Man's greatest need is to be reconciled to God, to have that broken relationship with God restored.

The Need for Reconciliation

God and man enjoyed a naturally close relationship in the beginning, but something ruined it. Man chose to violate the direct command of God. Consequently, the relationship was broken. Adam was our representative. When he sinned, we sinned. When he was driven out of God's presence, we were driven out of God's presence. The apostle Paul writes in Romans 3:23, "All have sinned and fall short of the glory of God." In Romans 5:12, we read, "Just as sin entered into the world through one man, and death through sin, and in this way death came to all people, because all sinned—"

Man has an enormous problem: God is holy, but we are sinful. God is righteous, but we are guilty. Being holy, God cannot tolerate sin. Therefore, one party must change. God is God. He will not change. Sinful man cannot become good enough or do enough good things to earn God's favor. In Isaiah 64:6, the prophet writes, "All of us have become like one who is unclean, and all our righteous acts are like filthy rags; we all shrivel up like a leaf, and like the wind our sins sweep us away." While we run from God, God runs toward us. He is the hound of heaven who chases down sinful man. Religion is man reaching up to God; biblical Christianity is God reaching down to man. If we cannot earn God's favor through church, baptism, charity, confirmation, or any other religious work, how, then, can we be reconciled to God? God's word gives the answer in Ephesians 2:8–9, as Paul writes, "It is by grace you have been saved, through faith—and this is not from yourselves, it is the gift of God—not by works, so that no one can boast."

Just as Adam was our representative through whom we inherited sin, so God provided another representative through whom we may inherit salvation and eternal life. This second Adam is Jesus Christ. He perfectly obeys where the first Adam failed. Acting in our place, his obedient life and sacrificial death restore us to a right relationship with God. Jesus restores us to God by doing three things:

1. Jesus is our substitute. The apostle Peter writes in 1 Peter 3:18, "Christ also suffered once for sins, the righteous for the unrighteous, to bring you to God." Jesus took our place on the cross, enduring the penalty that we deserved.

2. Jesus is our sacrifice of atonement. A "sacrifice of atonement" refers to the satisfaction of the demands of a righteous God, which is what Jesus did on the cross. The apostle Paul writes these words in Romans 3:23–25:

> All have sinned and fall short of the glory of God, and all are justified freely by his grace through the redemption that came by Christ Jesus. God presented Christ as a sacrifice of atonement, through the shedding of his blood—to be received by faith. He did this to demonstrate his righteousness.

Just as Adam and Eve were driven out of God's presence, so Christ was separated from his Father as a result of our sin. Near the end of three hours of darkness on the cross, during which the Father turned his back on his Son because of our sin, Jesus cried out, "It is finished" (John 19:30). The purpose for which he came to earth is accomplished. He pays our sin debt in full. He satisfies the demands of God's justice so we can be restored to God.

3. Jesus is our Redeemer. To "redeem" means to "buy back." This is what Jesus did when he died. He offered his lifeblood as the purchase price of our redemption. In Ephesians 1:7 we read, "In him we have redemption through his blood, the forgiveness of sins, in accordance with the riches of God's grace." Redemption transfers us. We are no longer outsiders, separated from God. Rather, Christ purchases us so that we are now citizens of God's kingdom.

Our Need for Reconciliation

God himself has provided the way to be reconciled to him. Reconciliation isn't automatic. Rather, God's word insists we must receive Christ's reconciling work by faith. John 3:36 makes it clear that "whoever believes in the Son has eternal life, but whoever rejects the Son will not see life, for God's wrath remains on them." This is difficult for us to accept. Our nature wants to earn everything we receive or refuse to see our need of it in the first place. God must bring us to the end of ourselves. We must see how helpless we really are. Funerals remind us of the fact that we are dependent on God for our every breath, whether we acknowledge that truth or not.

When you die and stand before your holy Creator, there will only be one issue. It is not which church you belonged to, or whether or not you were baptized or confirmed in your church, or whether you gave money to charity. The one issue will be this: "What did you do with Jesus Christ?" How, then, will you respond to God's love as demonstrated by his Son Jesus Christ?

In Psalm 39:4, we read, "Show me, LORD, my life's end and the number of my days; let me know how fleeting my life is." These words remind us that life on this earth is temporary and uncertain. It has been said that everything in life is uncertain except death. James, the brother of Jesus, reminds us of this when he writes, "You do not even know what will happen tomorrow. What is your life? You are a mist that appears for a little while and then vanishes" (James 4:14).

At times like these, when life's activities seem to come to a sudden halt, God would be pleased to see us pause and examine the state of our own souls. This solemn occasion reminds us of the uncertainty of life. Any of us may be called next. The question we must all ask ourselves is this: "Am I prepared?"

Peter Marshall, a Scottish-American preacher and chaplain of the United States Senate in the first half of the twentieth century, once told the following story:

> An old legend tells of a merchant in Baghdad who one day sent his servant to the market. Before very long the servant came back, white and trembling, and in great agitation said to his master: "Down in the market place I was jostled by a woman in the crowd, and when I turned around I saw it was Death that jostled me. She looked at me and made a threatening gesture. Master, please lend me your horse, for I must hasten away to avoid her. I will ride to Samarra and there I will hide, and Death will not find me."
>
> The merchant lent him his horse and the servant galloped away in great haste. Later the merchant went down to the market place and saw Death standing in the crowd. He went over to her and asked, "Why did you frighten my servant this morning? Why did you make a threatening gesture?"
>
> "That was not a threatening gesture," Death said. "It was only a start of surprise. I was astonished to see him in Baghdad, for I have an appointment with him tonight in Samarra."
>
> Each of us has an appointment in Samarra. But that is cause for rejoicing—not for fear, provided we have put our trust in him who alone holds the keys of life and death.[20]

Each of us has an appointment with God. In Hebrews 9:27, we are told that "people are destined to die once, and after that to face judgment." None of us know the day that has been appointed for us to die. The time to examine our own hearts is today. The Holy Spirit is saying to us, "Today, if you hear his voice, do not harden your hearts" (Hebrews 3:7–8). Every time we ignore or turn away from the truth of God's word, we harden our hearts. Today, God is graciously warning us that to do so is to take one more step toward our hearts being hardened forever. God wants reconciliation, not separation. He made us to enjoy fellowship with him. He has graciously given his Son, the Lord Jesus Christ, as his gift. I exhort you to come to God through him. In John 14:6, Jesus says, "I am the way and the truth and the life. No one comes to the Father except through me." There is no other way to God. "How shall we escape if we ignore so great a salvation?" (Hebrews 2:3).

CHAPTER 8

Sermon 3
GOD IS TRUSTWORTHY

> The secret things belong to the LORD our God, but the things revealed belong to us and to our children forever, that we may follow all the words of this law.
>
> Deuteronomy 29:29

> Small coffins are placed in the ground, but more than the body is buried.
>
> James W. Bruce III

WE THINK THAT IF ONLY WE KNOW MORE, we will worry less. If I knew what sort of college my child would be able to attend, I would worry less about their education. Perhaps. However, I would worry about other things—their health, their friendships, and so forth. We think knowing more means worrying less. In reality, we want to be like the One who has absolute knowledge of all things. The fact that we do not have absolute knowledge bothers us. It leads to anxiety, fear, and anger.

Our lack of absolute knowledge is felt when a loved one grows ill. Death makes us feel our finitude. The good news is that we will never have absolute knowledge. Nonetheless, we can also be freed from anxiety, fear, and anger because we belong to the God who has absolute knowledge. We may not know all things, but we know him who knows all things. In the face of sorrow and uncertainty, we cling to God and the truth he has given us to know. In Deuteronomy 29:29, we read these words: "The secret things belong to the LORD our God, but the things revealed belong to us and to our children forever, that we may follow all the words of this law." This verse teaches us three great truths about God.

Truth 1: God Keeps Some Things Secret.

The secret things that belong only to God include the divine purposes behind his divine decrees. We seldom understand God's ways because he who created the universe is infinite. Other parts of Scripture testify to this:

> "Remember the former things, those of long ago,
>> I am God, and there is no other;
>> I am God, and there is none like me.
> I make known the end from the beginning,
>> from ancient times, what is still to come.
> I say, 'My purpose will stand,
>> and I will do all that I please.'"

Isaiah 46:9–10

> Oh, the depth of the riches of the wisdom and knowledge
>> of God!
>> How unsearchable his judgments
>> and his paths beyond tracing out!

Romans 11:33

> Great is the LORD and most worthy of praise;
>> his greatness no one can fathom.

Psalm 145:3

> "For my thoughts are not your thoughts,
>> neither are your ways my ways,"
>> declares the LORD.
> "As the heavens are higher than the earth,
>> so are my ways higher than your ways
>> and my thoughts than your thoughts."

Isaiah 55:8–9

It is clear that God's thoughts and purposes are infinitely above our own. In our limited human minds, we do not understand why God created Seth, the longed-for child of a couple in our church, and then chose to end his life before we could have the joy of knowing him. But that is OK. God doesn't call us to live in the realm of the secret things; he calls us to rest in his unchanging nature and character. He is the sovereign One. He calls us to stand on him, for he is, as the psalmist reminds us in Psalm 46, "our refuge and strength, our ever-present help in trouble."

There is a second truth before us.

Truth 2: God Has Revealed What It Is Necessary for Us to Know.

Deuteronomy 29:29 tells us that the secret things belong to God, and then it goes on to declare that "the things revealed belong to us and to our children forever." Although there are some things we will never know, there is a great deal that we do know. Let us set aside what we cannot understand and focus on what God has revealed in the Bible concerning all that we need to know.

1. We know that *God only does what is good.*

Good and upright is the LORD;
    therefore he instructs sinners in his ways.
He guides the humble in what is right
    and teaches them his way.
All the ways of the LORD are loving and faithful
    toward those who keep the demands of his covenant.

Psalm 25:8-10

Every good and perfect gift is from above, coming down from the Father of the heavenly lights, who does not change like shifting shadows.

James 1:17

2. We know that *God only does what is holy.*

Exalt the LORD our God
    and worship at his holy mountain,
    for the LORD our God is holy.

Psalm 99:9

Being holy, God is totally distinct from all his creatures. God is completely without sin or defilement of any kind.

3. We know that *God only does what is right.*

The LORD is righteous in all his ways
    and faithful in all he does.

Psalm 145:17

God always does what he knows is right. He never makes mistakes. Whether or not we fully understand his ways is not important; what is important is that by faith we know that God is righteous and kind, and therefore we cling to that truth.

4. We know that *God created us to enjoy him*.

Bring my sons from afar
    and my daughters from the ends of the earth—
everyone who is called by my name,
    whom I created for my glory,
    whom I formed and made.

Isaiah 43:6–7

God created man in order to pour out his love on him, and when man finds complete joy and satisfaction in his Creator, God is glorified. Having created Adam and Eve in his image, the triune Godhead enjoyed fellowship with man.

5. We know that *we are broken*.

In the beginning, God created man from the dust of the earth and breathed into him the breath of life. As creatures made in the image of God, man and woman enjoyed a unique relationship with their Creator God. God told them this intimate fellowship would continue as long as they remained obedient to his command not to eat from the tree of the knowledge of good and evil. If they disobeyed, they would surely die. Man and woman chose to rebel against God's clear command, and death came as a result. Spiritual death came—immediately they knew they were no longer at peace with God. Physical death also came—God killed an animal and made clothing out of the skins. This was the first sign that God would accept a sacrifice for sin. And we read in Genesis 5:5 that Adam and Eve's own physical lives also later came to an end.

6. We know that *God's Son came to reconcile us to God.*

Jesus is called "the Lamb of God" because he was sent by God to be the perfect sacrifice for sin, to die so that men and women could live. As he hung on the cross, Jesus took the penalty of our sin on himself, thus becoming our sacrifice. His death now brings us life. First Peter 3:18 reads, "Christ also suffered once for sins, the righteous for the unrighteous, to bring you to God. He was put to death in the body but made alive in the Spirit." Since God is holy, he requires a just sacrifice. Since we are unjust, our sacrifice is unacceptable. So the perfect Son of God became a man. Being man, he could die in man's place as his substitute. And, being God, he could die as the perfect sacrifice, acceptable to God. In light of the cross of Jesus, it is right to conclude that no one understands suffering like Jesus does. And no one understands the grief of losing a child to death more deeply than the heavenly Father.

Because of this truth, a wondrous exchange takes place the moment a person turns from his or her sin to trust in Christ for salvation. In 2 Corinthians 5:21, the apostle Paul writes, "God made him who had no sin to be sin for us, so that in him we might become the righteousness of God." As the sinner's substitute, Christ allowed the weight of our guilt to be placed on him on the cross. God the Father then poured out his righteous wrath on his Son, offering sacrifice for sin "once for all," as Hebrews 10:10 reminds us.

When we as sinners turn to God in repentance, trusting in the sacrifice of Christ on our behalf, God forgives our sin and credits the righteousness of Christ to us, and we are justified. As our substitute, Christ died to satisfy God's justice and to demonstrate his love. The apostle Paul, in Romans 5:6–8, writes these words:

> You see, at just the right time, when we were still powerless, Christ died for the ungodly. Very rarely will anyone die for a righteous person; though for a good person someone might possibly dare to die. But God demonstrates his own love for us in this: While we were still sinners, Christ died for us.

7. We know that *we have eternal life in Christ.*

Death is often viewed as the end, but it is not. The main message of the Bible is that the death, burial, and resurrection of Christ bring hope to sinners. In Romans 6:23, Paul writes, "The wages of sin is death, but the gift of God is eternal life in Christ Jesus our Lord." While grieving the death of his infant son, King David said, "But now that he is dead, why should I go on fasting? Can I bring him back again? I will go to him, but he will not return to me" (2 Samuel 12:23). Seth's parents possess this same confidence and hope because their trust is in Jesus Christ as Lord and Savior. Knowing Christ means they have an eternal home in heaven; it also means they will see Seth again.

Our verse contains a third truth.

Truth 3: God Holds Us Accountable for How We Respond to His Revealed Truth.

Deuteronomy 29:29 declares, "The secret things belong to the LORD our God, but the things revealed belong to us and to our children forever"; however, the verse concludes with these words: "that we may follow all the words of this law." God doesn't call us to understand the secret things that belong to him; he only expects us to respond to the truth that he has revealed to us in the Scriptures.

My friends, you have been summoned here today by God. It is no accident that Seth's short life has ended. It is no accident that you are sitting here tonight listening to God's word. My question to you is not, "Do you understand why God has chosen to do what he has done?" but rather, "How will you respond to the spiritual truth God has revealed to you in his word?"

God has provided salvation through his Son, Jesus Christ. All who will come to him in repentant faith are forgiven, stand justified before their holy Creator, and will one day spend eternity in his presence. All who reject him already stand condemned and will only see God's face in the final judgment.

When something happens that we do not understand, we have a choice. We can demand to know the secret things, doubt God, and perhaps even become angry and bitter against him. Or we can acknowledge our limited understanding, surrender to God, and trust him. We do not know everything, but we do know we have a God who can be trusted to make no mistakes. He is holy and righteous and good, and in this we rejoice.

At the age of twenty-seven, Ron Hamilton underwent exploratory surgery for a problem he was having with his left eye. The doctors discovered cancer and removed the eye. The song "Rejoice in the Lord" was born out of this experience:

God never moves without purpose or plan,
When trying His servant and molding a man.

Comfort the Grieving

Give thanks to the Lord though your testing seems long;
In darkness He giveth a song.

I could not see through the shadows ahead;
So I looked at the cross of my Savior instead.
I bowed to the will of the Master that day;
Then peace came and tears fled away.

Now I can see testing comes from above;
God strengthens His children and purges in love.
My Father knows best, and I trust in His care;
Through purging, more fruit I will bear.

Chorus:
O rejoice in the Lord, He makes no mistake.
He knoweth the end of each path that I take.
For when I am tried and purified,
I shall come forth as gold.[21]

ACKNOWLEDGMENTS

I THANK THE PATIENT FLOCK that God called me to shepherd—Immanuel Bible Church in Sheboygan, Wisconsin—for allowing me to show my frail humanity by grieving with them in times of earthly loss. I am especially grateful to the following:

- Jerome Pitz, for being supportive of my desire to dedicate this book to the memory of his wife, Jean, and to include portions of her memorial service
- Jackie Arnoldi, for giving me permission to share the poem she wrote in honor of her mother
- William and Carolyn Freel, for their willingness to let me include the Bible meditation given at their newborn son's memorial service
- Ken Dolezal, for permitting me to include a personal letter to a grieving brother
- Jonathan Allston, for allowing me to share the lyrics to his song "O Refuge Near"—a fitting theme for this book.

I thank hospice nurse and author Deborah Howard for her helpful comments and suggestions. Since she ministers to the dying on a daily basis and has written on the subject of grief ministry, her input has been invaluable. During my first few years of pastoral ministry, God, in his providence, first exposed me to hospice services, through which I have witnessed a side of the dying process that I had not seen before. As a result, I have grown to appreciate those who give themselves to this invaluable service.

I thank my faithful wife, Karen, for her constant support and encouragement. Heaven alone knows the sacrifices she has made for the sake of the Lord's church. Her reward will be greater than mine. I have truly been favored by the Lord (Proverbs 18:22).

SCRIPTURES THAT COMFORT

PRINT THE FOLLOWING LISTS double-sided and laminate them. Keep them in your wallet for your own use; also keep a supply on hand to give to family and friends who are ministering to their loved ones.

Food for the Soul
When in need of strength — Psalm 46
When in fear — Psalm 23
When discouraged — Isaiah 40
When filled with anxiety — Matthew 6:19–34
When bitterness has set in — 1 Corinthians 13:1–7
When life seems bigger than God — Psalm 90
When God seems distant — Psalm 139
When in need of peace and rest — Matthew 11:25–30
The secret of happiness — Matthew 5:1–9
For a description of heaven — Revelation 21

Food for the Soul

When in need of mercy—Psalm 103
When concerned about forgiveness—Psalm 51:1–13
When concerned about eternal life—John 3:1–21
Who is Jesus Christ?—John 20:30–31; 1 John 5:11–13
Why did Jesus come?—Isaiah 53; Romans 5
God's plan of salvation—Ephesians 2:1–10
Christ our Mediator—1 Timothy 2:5–6
When concerned about faith—Hebrews 11
God's unfailing love—Romans 8:31–39
The goodness of God—Psalm 111

POETRY, SONGS, AND PRAYERS

The Unsearchable Ways of God

In memory of Rachel M. Matt

Sometimes God's ways are hard to understand;
We want to ask "Why," to follow His hand.
Sometimes when tragedy comes from above,
It tempts us to waver, to doubt His love.
But God is infinitely wise and good,
He is too lofty to be understood.
His love is endless; His kindness is great.
He is too wise to leave one thing to fate.
Though His purpose may be unknown to us,
We cling to the Rock; in Him we must trust.
To Him we can run; with Him we can plead,
An ever-present help in time of need.
Our hearts they ache, our minds they probe,
But ultimately we must learn from Job.
The Lord who gives can also take away,
His name must be blessed each and every day.
We may wonder why He would make us weep;
His ways unsearchable, His knowledge deep.
So freely cry, tears and grief are His gifts,

Comfort the Grieving

By His grace He heals, by His strength He lifts.[22]

Paul Tautges, based on Romans 11:33;
Psalm 46:1; 18:2; Job 1:21

Whate'er My God Ordains Is Right

Whate'er my God ordains is right:
His holy will abideth;
I will be still whate'er He doth;
And follow where He guideth;
He is my God; though dark my road,
He holds me that I shall not fall:
Wherefore to Him I leave it all.

Whate'er my God ordains is right:
He is my Friend and Father;
He suffers naught to do me harm,
Though many storms may gather;
Now I may know both joy and woe,
Someday I shall see clearly
That He hath loved me dearly.

Whate'er my God ordains is right:
Though now this cup, in drinking,
May bitter seem to my faint heart,
I take it, all unshrinking.
My God is true; each morn anew
Sweet comfort yet shall fill my heart,
And pain and sorrow shall depart.[23]

Samuel Rodigast, 1676

Jesus, Lover of My Soul

Jesus, Lover of my soul, let me to Thy bosom fly,
While the nearer waters roll, while the tempest still is high.
Hide me, O my Savior, hide, till the storm of life is past;
Safe into the haven guide, O receive my soul at last!

Other refuge have I none, hangs my helpless soul on Thee;
Leave, O leave me not alone, still support and comfort me.
All my trust on Thee is stayed, all my help from Thee
  I bring;
Cover my defenseless head with the shadow of Thy wing.

Thou, O Christ, art all I want; more than all in Thee I find.
Raise the fallen, cheer the faint, heal the sick, and lead
  the blind.
Just and holy is Thy name; I am all unrighteousness;
False and full of sin I am, Thou art full of truth and grace.

Plenteous grace with Thee is found, grace to cover all my sin;
Let the healing streams abound; make me, keep me pure
  within.
Thou of life the fountain art, freely let me take of Thee;
Spring Thou up within my heart, rise to all eternity.

Charles Wesley, 1740

Children of the Heavenly Father

Children of the heavenly Father safely in His bosom gather;
Nestling bird nor star in heaven such a refuge e'er was given.

God His own doth tend and nourish, in His holy courts
  they flourish;

Comfort the Grieving

From all evil things He spares them, in His mighty arms
    He bears them.

Neither life nor death shall ever from the Lord His children
    sever;
Unto them His grace He showeth, and their sorrows all He
    knoweth.

Though He giveth or He taketh, God His children ne'er
    forsaketh;
His the loving purpose solely to preserve them pure and holy.

Lo, their very hairs He numbers, and no daily care encumbers
Them that share His ev'ry blessing and His help in woes
    distressing.

Praise the Lord in joyful numbers, Your Protector never slumbers;
At the will of your Defender ev'ry foeman must surrender.

> Karolina W. Sandell-Berg, 1858 (translated from
> Swedish into English by Ernst Olson in 1925)

Come, Ye Disconsolate

Come, ye disconsolate,* where'er ye languish,
Come to the mercy-seat, fervently kneel;
Here bring your wounded hearts, here tell your anguish;
"Earth has no sorrows that heaven cannot heal."

Joy of the desolate, Light of the straying,
Hope of the penitent, fadeless and pure!
Here speaks the Comforter, in mercy saying,
"Earth has no sorrows that heaven cannot cure."

---

*The word *disconsolate* means "sad beyond comforting."

Here see the bread of life; see waters flowing
Forth from the throne of God, pure from above.
Come to the feast prepared; come, ever knowing
"Earth has no sorrows but heaven can remove."

Thomas Moore, 1816; stanza 3
by Thomas Hastings, 1832

Heaven Desired

O my Lord,
   May I arrive where means of grace cease
      and I need no more to fast, pray, weep, watch,
      be tempted, attend preaching and sacrament;
      where nothing defiles,
      where is no grief, sorrow, sin, death, separation, tears,
         pale face, languid body, aching joints, feeble infancy,
         decrepit age, peccant humours, pining sickness,
         griping fears, consuming cares;
      where is personal completeness;
      where the more perfect the sight the more beautiful
         the object,
         the more perfect the appetite the sweeter the food,
         the more musical the ear the more pleasant the
           melody,
         the more complete the soul the more happy
           its joys,
   where is full knowledge of thee.
Here I am an ant, and as I view a nest of ants
   so dost thou view me and my fellow-creatures;
But as an ant knows not me, my nature, my thoughts,

Comfort the Grieving

so here I cannot know thee clearly.
But there I shall be near thee,
dwell with my family,
stand in thy presence chamber,
be an heir of thy kingdom,
as the spouse of Christ,
as a member of his body,
one with him who is with thee,
and exercise all my powers of body and soul
in the enjoyment of thee.
As praise in the mouth of thy saints is comely,
so teach me to exercise this divine gift,
when I pray, read, hear, see, do,
in the presence of people and of my enemies,
as I hope to praise thee eternally hereafter.[24]

Author unknown

Under His Wings

Under His wings I am safely abiding,
Tho' the night deepens and tempests are wild,
Still I can trust Him—I know He will keep me,
He has redeemed me and I am His child.

Under His wings, what a refuge in sorrow!
How the heart yearningly turns to His rest!
Often when earth has no balm for my healing,
There I find comfort and there I am blest.

Under His wings, O what precious enjoyment!
There will I hide till life's trials are o'er;

Sheltered, protected, no evil can harm me,
Resting in Jesus I'm safe evermore.

Chorus:
Under His wings, under His wings, who from His love
    can sever?
Under His wings my soul shall abide, safely abide forever.

William O. Cushing, 1924

Consolation

How sweet amid earth's wild alarms, to feel the everlasting arms;
To know He careth day by day, and will not turn our prayer away.

He hears our plea, He sends relief, He gives us solace from our grief;
He sends refreshing showers down, and thus our lives with
    blessings crown.

We'll abide in Him, then every hour, and we will feel His
    sovereign power;
He'll be our strength, our refuge sweet, and all our faith He
    will complete.

Oh, let our prayers like incense rise unto the Lord of earth and skies;
Give thanks for all His mercy shown, praise Him who claims us
    for His own.

Georgie Tillman Snead, 1929

Sovereign Ruler of the Skies

Sovereign Ruler of the skies, ever gracious, ever wise,
All my times are in Thy hand, all events at Thy command.

Comfort the Grieving

He that formed me in the womb, He shall guide me to
    the tomb.
All my times shall ever be ordered by his wise decree.

Times of sickness, times of health; times of poverty and
    of wealth;
Times of trial and times of grief; times of triumph and relief;
Times the tempter's power to prove; times to taste a Savior's
    love.
All must come, and last, and end, as shall please my heavenly
    Friend.

Plagues and deaths around me fly; till he bids, I cannot die;
Not a single dart can hit, till the God of love thinks fit.
O Thou gracious, wise, and just, in Thy hands my life I trust;
Thee at all times will I bless: having Thee I all possess.

John Ryland, 1777

The Way of the Cross Leads Home

I must needs go home by the way of the cross,
There's no other way but this;
I shall ne'er get sight of the Gates of Light,
If the way of the cross I miss.

I must needs go on in the blood-sprinkled way,
The path that the Savior trod,
If I ever climb to the heights sublime,
Where the soul is at home with God.

Then I bid farewell to the way of the world,
To walk in it nevermore;

For my Lord says, "Come," and I seek my home,
Where He waits at the open door.

Chorus:
The way of the cross leads home,
The way of the cross leads home;
It is sweet to know, as I onward go,
The way of the cross leads home.

Jesse B. Pounds, 1906

O Refuge Near

O refuge near, our strength in weakness, forever in His
    hands secure;
Emmanuel, God always with us, Almighty One within
    my soul.
I'll never fear the roaring waters; the tempests know the One
    in me.
The hands that hold the stars in motion are holding me in
    love and care.

Consider well His lovingkindness; He never will your soul
    forsake.
Find rest in Him; yet in your resting, spend all your strength
    for Jesus' sake.
Look on His face, so bruised and bleeding; look on His soul
    that knew no sin.
The God of love was pleased to wound Him when our soul's
    sins were laid on Him.

Are you too strong to rest in His strength, or is your mind
    too wise for Him?

Comfort the Grieving

Do riches bring more love and mercy than Jesus Christ the
  perfect Lamb?
Does He who made you lack in power or He who died too
  short on love?
Can you think on those nails run through His hands and
  claim He's not enough for you?

My dearest Lord, Your love o'erwhelms me; my cup can't
  hold the gifts You give.
The pages of my life are empty for You to fill just as
  You wish.
I want for You to write my story; blot out the words that I
  have penned.
Fill every page for Your own glory and end it with the words,
  "Well done!"[25]

Jonathan Allston

Lord, You Are My Everything

Lord, You are my Comfort.
When hard times come my way,
Your presence never leaves me.
You are with me all the way.

Lord, You are my Strength.
When I grow weary in this land,
Never will I falter.
I'm upheld by Your right hand.

Lord, You are my Peace.
You are the calmer of my fears.

Poetry, Songs, and Prayers

When worries overwhelm me,
Your love wipes away my tears.

Lord, You're my Sustainer,
You hold me safely at Your side.
I will make it through the storms,
Because in You I will abide.

Lord, You are my Joy.
Amidst the trials and the pain,
I trust Your sovereign care.
I see the Son between the rain.

Lord, You are my Rock,
My firm foundation, solid ground.
You are mighty and unchanging,
You have no limits and no bounds.

Lord, You are my Everything,
Life with You is so complete.
One day You'll bring me home to You,
And I will worship at Your feet.[26]

> Jackie Arnoldi, dedicated to my mom,
> Jean Pitz, whose Lord was her everything,
> June 9, 1953–April 12, 2008

SAMPLE MEMORIAL SERVICES

AS A GENERAL RULE, memorial services should be on the brief side. The bereaved are exhausted from the numerous decisions of previous days—and sometimes months or even years in the case of prolonged sickness. Therefore, their attention spans will not be long. However, the minister who is responsible for officiating must also ensure that the service is substantial enough to properly honor the deceased and recognize the value of the life that has been lived. Sherwin Nuland writes, "The greatest dignity to be found in death is the dignity of the life that preceded it."[27] Because of the sanctity of human life, memorial services must always be handled with utmost dignity and respect.

The following are some sample orders of service for the funerals of both unbelievers and believers.

When the Deceased Is Likely an Unbeliever
Sample 1

Prelude
Welcome Thank you for being here today to share in this special service in honor of _____. We have come to express our final good-byes to a wife, mother, grandmother, relative, and friend who has impacted all of our lives in some way.

Obituary
Scripture Psalm 27
Prayer
Special memories from family
Song "The Lord's Prayer" (Matthew 6:9–13;
music by Albert Hay Malotte;
arr. Donald Hustad, 1953)
Scripture Psalm 90
Message "The God of Grace Pursues Reconciliation"
(see chapter 7)
Prayer
Song "How Great Thou Art"
(Carl Gustav Boberg; trans. Stuart K. Hine)
(Funeral director to close the service with instructions.)

Sample 2

This service is designed for a military veteran and is particularly appropriate in the United States. The principles on which the service is based can be applied more generally to recognize the achievements of people in other fields of service.

Prelude
Welcome Thank you for being here today to share
in this special service in memory of one of our veterans,
_____. Let's take a few moments to reflect on John's life.
Obituary
Scripture Psalm 46
Prayer
Song a patriotic hymn

Comfort the Grieving

Message "The God of Grace Brings Life Out of Death"
(see chapter 6)
Prayer
Song: "America, the Beautiful" (Katharine Lee Bates)
**(Funeral director to close the service with
thank-you and announcements.)**

When the Deceased Is a Believer
Sample 1

Song "Amazing Grace" (John Newton)
Welcome Thank you for being here today to share in this
special service in honor of _____. As we reflect on the part
that _____ played in each of our lives, let us remember
some of the highlights of his [her] life.
Obituary based on the outline given in Ecclesiastes 3:1 – 8
Scripture Psalm 46
Prayer
Song "O the Deep, Deep Love of Jesus"
(Samuel Trevor Francis)
Message "Lessons from the Death of Lazarus"
(based on John 11; sermon not included in this book)
Prayer
Scripture 1 Thessalonians 4:13 – 18
Song "How Great Thou Art" (Carl Gustav Boberg;
trans. Stuart K. Hine)
**(Funeral director to close the service with
thank-you and announcements.)**

Sample 2

(This memorial service was in honor of Jean Pitz, who fought a courageous battle against cancer prior to receiving the eternal reward of her faith. It is longer than a typical service because of the breadth of her influence in the church and because we wanted to honor the desires of her family.)

Song "God Makes No Mistakes" (Mac and Beth Lynch)

Welcome

Obituary based on the outline given in Ecclesiastes 3:1–8

Scripture John 11:1–36

Prayer

Congregational hymn "Rejoice in the Lord"
(Ron Hamilton)

Congregational hymn "When We See Christ"
(Esther Kerr Rusthoi)

Special memories from family

Message "The God of Grace Saves Sinners" (see chapter 7)

Ministry of music "It Is Not Death to Die"
(H. A. César Malan; trans. George W. Bethune)

Scripture 1 John 5:11–13

Congregational hymn "In Christ Alone"
(Keith Getty and Stuart Townend)

Closing prayer

RECOMMENDED RESOURCES

Resources to Strengthen Pastoral Ministry and Counseling

Baxter, Richard. *The Reformed Pastor*. 1656. Reprint, Edinburgh: Banner of Truth, 1974.

Bridges, Charles. *The Christian Ministry*. 1830. Reprint, Edinburgh: Banner of Truth, 1967.

Croft, Brian, and Cara Croft. *The Pastor's Family*. Grand Rapids: Zondervan, 2013.

Dever, Mark. *Nine Marks of a Healthy Church*. Wheaton, IL: Crossway, 2004.

Duncan, J. Ligon, and Susan Hunt. *Women's Ministry in the Local Church*. Wheaton, IL: Crossway, 2006.

Elliff, Tom. *A Passion for Prayer*. Wheaton, IL: Crossway, 1998.

Kuiper, R. B. *God-Centered Evangelism*. London: Banner of Truth, 1966.

MacArthur, John, and the Master's Seminary Faculty. *Rediscovering Pastoral Ministry*. Dallas: Word, 1995.

Nettles, Thomas J. *By His Grace and for His Glory*. Lake Charles, LA: Cor Meum Tibi, 2002.

Piper, John. *Brothers, We Are Not Professionals*. Nashville: B & H, 2002.

Recommended Resources

Powlison, David. *Seeing with New Eyes*. Phillipsburg, NJ: P & R, 2003.

———— *Speaking Truth in Love: Counsel in Community*. Winston-Salem, NC: Punch Press, 2005.

————, ed. *The Journal of Biblical Counseling on CD-ROM, Version 2.0*. Glenside, PA: Christian Counseling & Educational Foundation, 1977–2005.

Shaw, John. *The Character of a Pastor According to God's Heart*. Ligonier, PA: Soli Deo Gloria, 1992.

Spurgeon, Charles H. *An All-Round Ministry*. Pasadena, TX: Pilgrim, 1983.

Thomas, Curtis C. *Life in the Body of Christ*. Cape Coral, FL: Founders, 2006.

Watson, Thomas. *A Body of Divinity*. 1692. Reprint, London: Banner of Truth, 1965.

Resources on Grief, Comfort, and the Sovereignty of God in Suffering

Baxter, Richard. *Dying Thoughts*. 1683. Reprint, Edinburgh: Banner of Truth, 2004.

Bridges, Jerry. *Trusting God*. Colorado Springs: NavPress, 1988.

Bruce, James W., III. *From Grief to Glory: A Book of Comfort for Grieving Parents*. Edinburgh: Banner of Truth, 2008. Visit his website at www.grieftoglory.com.

Edwards, Jonathan. *Heaven: A World of Love*. Edinburgh: Banner of Truth, 2008.

Howard, Deborah. *Sunsets: Reflections for Life's Final Journey*. Wheaton, IL: Crossway, 2005.

Comfort the Grieving

Kaiser, Walter C. *Grief and Pain in the Plan of God*. Fearn, Scotland: Christian Focus, 2004.

Kellemen, Robert W. *God's Healing for Life's Losses*. Winona Lake, IN: BMH, 2010.

Ketcham, R. T. *Christ: The Comforter in Sorrow*. Schaumburg, IL: Regular Baptist Press, n.d.

Piper, John, and Justin Taylor, eds. *Suffering and the Sovereignty of God*. Wheaton, IL: Crossway, 2006.

Tripp, Paul David. *Grief: Finding Hope Again*. Greensboro, NC: New Growth, 2004.

Poetry, Prayers, and Hymn Stories

Bennett, Arthur, ed. *The Valley of Vision*. Edinburgh: Banner of Truth, 1975.

MacArthur, John, Joni Eareckson Tada, and Robert and Bobbie Wolgemuth. *O Worship the King: Hymns of Assurance and Praise to Encourage Your Heart*. Wheaton, IL: Crossway, 2000.

———. *When Morning Gilds the Skies: Hymns of Heaven and Our Eternal Hope*. Wheaton, IL: Crossway, 2002.

Moments with the Book: www.mwtb.org.

Morgan, Robert J. *Then Sings My Soul: 150 of the World's Greatest Hymn Stories*. Nashville: Thomas Nelson, 2003.

Osbeck, Kenneth. *101 Hymn Stories*. Grand Rapids: Kregel, 1982.

———. *101 More Hymn Stories*. Grand Rapids: Kregel, 1985.

Standfield, Anne. *Seasons of Comfort and Joy*. Leominster, UK: Day One, 2008.

Recommended Resources

Websites with Biblical Counseling Resources

Association of Biblical Counselors: www.christiancounseling.com

Association of Certified Biblical Counselors: biblical
counseling.com

Biblical Counseling Center: biblicalcounselingcenter.org

Biblical Counseling Coalition: bccoalition.org

Center for Pastoral Life and Care: christiancounseling
.com/cplc

Christian Counsel & Educational Foundation: ccef.org

Counseling One Another: counselingoneanother.com

Faith Biblical Counseling: faithlafayette.org

Grief to Glory: grieftoglory.com

Institute for Biblical Counseling and Discipleship: ibcd.org

Strengthening Ministries: mackministries.org

Women Helping Women: elysefitzpatrick.com

NOTES

1. Paul David Tripp, *Grief: Finding Hope Again* (Greensboro, NC: New Growth, 2004), 8.
2. Warren W. Wiersbe, *Be Comforted* (Wheaton, IL: Scripture Press, 1992), 7.
3. Joni Eareckson Tada and Steve Estes, *When God Weeps* (Grand Rapids: Zondervan, 1997), 202.
4. Deborah Howard, *Sunsets: Reflections for Life's Final Journey* (Wheaton, IL: Crossway, 2005), 35. All italics within nonscriptural quotations are the original writer's. Italicized words or phrases within Scripture quotations indicate emphasis added by this author.
5. "How Firm a Foundation," "K—" in John Rippon's *A Selection of Hymns from the Best Authors* (1787).
6. Dustin Shramek, "Waiting for the Morning during the Long Night of Weeping," in *Suffering and the Sovereignty of God*, ed. John Piper and Justin Taylor (Wheaton, IL: Crossway, 2006), 189.
7. James W. Bruce III, *From Grief to Glory: A Book of Comfort for Grieving Parents* (Edinburgh: Banner of Truth, 2008), 70–71. In the providence of God, I came across this book one week prior to my first publication deadline for this book. I highly recommend you purchase copies as gifts for parents who have lost children. If you do not know anyone in this situation now, buy a few copies anyway to keep on hand for when you do meet such people. The death of children is more common than we realize.
8. Walter C. Kaiser Jr., *Grief and Pain in the Plan of God* (Fearn, Scotland: Christian Focus, 2004), 43, emphasis added.
9. Quoted in Michael Green, *Illustrations for Biblical Preaching* (Grand Rapids: Baker, 1982), 406.
10. Author unknown; used by permission. Every pastor should have a supply of this tract-size poem to place inside sympathy cards or to use on personal visits. I have used it for more than a decade, and it has brought much encouragement to sufferers. It is published by a literature ministry called Moments with the Book; check out their great selection of comforting poems at www.mwtb.org.
11. Paul David Tripp, *Grief: Finding Hope Again* (Greensboro, NC: New Growth, 2010), 4.
12. C. H. Spurgeon, "The Hope Laid Up in Heaven," in *Classic Sermons on Hope*, ed. Warren W. Wiersbe (Grand Rapids: Kregel, 1994), 125.
13. B. B. Warfield, "The Emotional Life of Our Lord," available at

Notes

www.monergism.com/thethreshold/articles/onsite/emotionallife.html (accessed June 23, 2014).

14. Kevin Ruffcorn, "Grief Aftercare: Care Begins before the Funeral and Continues during the Following Months," Christianity Today International, available at www.salvationarmy.org.nz/uploads/file/Care%20 for%20a%20family%20with%20a%20Death%20of%20a%20Child.pdf (accessed June 2, 2014).

15. Tripp, Grief, 11.

16. Shramek, "Waiting for the Morning," 177.

17. Howard, Sunsets, 43.

18. Robert W. Kellemen, God's Healing for Life's Losses: How to Find Hope When You're Hurting (Winona Lake, IN: BMH, 2010), 7.

19. Kiron K. Skinner, Annelise Anderson, and Martin Anderson, eds., Reagan: A Life in Letters (New York: Free Press, 2003), ix.

20. Cited in Haddon Robinson, Biblical Sermons: How Twelve Preachers Apply the Principles of Biblical Preaching (Grand Rapids: Baker, 1997), 177.

21. Ron Hamilton ("Patch the Pirate"), "Rejoice in the Lord." Copyright © 1978, by Majesty Music, Inc. Used by permission.

22. Taken from Paul Tautges, Delight in the Word (Enumclaw, WA: Pleasant Word, 2007), 80–81.

23. Taken from Trinity Hymnal. Used by permission of Great Commission Publications. All rights reserved.

24. Taken from The Valley of Vision © Copyright 1975 by Arthur Bennett. Published by The Banner of Truth Trust, Edinburgh, www.banneroftruth .org. Used by permission of the publisher.

25. Jonathan Allston, "O Refuge Near" (previously unpublished hymn). Used by permission.

26. Jackie Arnoldi, "Lord, You Are My Everything" (previously unpublished poem). Used by permission.

27. Sherwin Nuland, How We Die: Reflections on Life's Final Chapter (New York: Random House, 2010), 242.

Practical
Shepherding

The Practical Shepherding series provides pastors and ministry leaders with practical help to do the work of pastoral ministry in a local church. The seven-volume series, when complete, will include:

- *Conduct Gospel-Centered Funerals: Applying the Gospel at the Unique Challenges of Death*

- *Prepare Them to Shepherd: Test, Train, Affirm, and Send the Next Generation of Pastors*

- *Visit the Sick: Ministering God's Grace in Times of Illness*

- *Comfort the Grieving: Ministering God's Grace in Times of Loss*

- *Gather God's People: Understand, Plan, and Lead Worship in Your Local Church*

- *Pray for the Flock: Ministering God's Grace through Intercession* (Available August 2015)

- *Exercise Oversight: Shepherding the Flock through Administration and Delegation* (Available August 2015)

In addition to the series, be sure to look for these titles by Brian and Cara Croft on the pastor's family and ministry:

- *The Pastor's Family* by Brian and Cara Croft

- *The Pastor's Ministry* by Brian Croft (Available April 2015)